From Analyst to Leader

Elevating the Role of the
Business Analyst

From Analyst to Leader

Elevating the Role of the Business Analyst

Kathleen B. Hass, PMP

With Contributions from
Richard Vander Horst, PMP
Kimi Ziemski, PMP

With an Epilogue from
Lori Lindbergh, PMP

MANAGEMENTCONCEPTS

**(((**
MANAGEMENTCONCEPTS

8230 Leesburg Pike, Suite 800
Vienna, VA 22182
703.790.9595
Fax: 703.790.1371
www.managementconcepts.com

Printed in the United States of America

Library of Congress Cataloging-in-Publication Data

Hass, Kathleen B.
From analyst to leader : elevating the role of the business analyst / Kathleen B. Hass; with contributions from Richard Vander Horst, Kimi Ziemski; with an epilogue from Lori Lindbergh,.
    p. cm. -- (Business analysis essential library)
ISBN 978-1-56726-213-1
    1. Business analysts. 2. Project management--Decision making.
            3. Business requirements analysis. 4. Self-directed work teams.
            I. Vander Horst, Richard. II. Ziemski, Kimi. III. Title.
HD69.B87H37 2008
658.4'092—dc22

                                                                        2007035266

10   9   8   7   6   5   4   3   2   1

About the Authors

Kathleen Hass, PMP, is the Project Management and Business Analysis Practice Leader for Management Concepts. Ms. Hass is a prominent presenter at industry conferences and is an author and lecturer in strategic project management and business analysis disciplines. Her expertise includes leading technology and software-intensive projects, building and leading strategic project teams, and conducting program management for large, complex engagements. Ms. Hass has more than 25 years of experience in project management and business analysis, including project portfolio management implementation, project office creation and management, business process reengineering, IT applications development and technology deployment, project management and business analysis training and mentoring, and requirements management. Ms. Hass has managed large, complex projects in the airline, telecommunications, retail, and manufacturing industries, and in the U.S. federal government.

Ms. Hass' consulting experience includes engagements with multiple agencies within the federal government, such as USDA, USGS, NARA, and an agency within the intelligence community, as well as industry engagements at Colorado Springs Utilities, Toyota Financial Services, Toyota Motor Sales, the Salt Lake Organizing Committee for the 2002 Olympic Winter Games, Hilti US Inc., The SABRE Group, Sulzer Medica, and Qwest Communications. Client services have included maturity assessments, project quality and risk assessment, project launches, troubled project recovery, risk management, and implementation of program management offices, strategic planning, and project portfolio management processes.

Ms. Hass earned a B.A. in business administration with summa cum laude honors from Western Connecticut University.

Lori Lindbergh, MBA, PMP, is president of Lindbergh Consulting and has more than 20 years of experience in general management, project management, and organizational assessment. Ms. Lindbergh has consulted with organizations in the healthcare, telecommunications, information technology, energy, pharmaceutical, and financial services industries, and in the federal government.

Ms. Lindbergh's educational accomplishments include an M.B.A. from the University of Baltimore and a B.S. in nursing from Eastern Kentucky University. She is currently completing her Ph.D. in industrial/organizational psychology at Capella University. Her upcoming dissertation will attempt to quantify how key factors in the organizational environment affect project manager self-efficacy and project outcomes.

Richard Vander Horst, MBA, PMP, has worked in information technology for Wegmans Food Markets for over 17 years. As a supervisor for the project support services, he oversees a variety of business analysis, project management, and portfolio planning support activities. Mr. Vander Horst is also a member of the board of directors and a co-founder of mpXML, a meat and poultry data standards organization.

Mr. Vander Horst is a member of the Project Management Institute, and a member of the International Institute of Business Analysis. He earned a B.S. in finance and a M.B.A from St. John Fisher College.

Kimi Ziemski, PMP, is an experienced project account manager and marketing professional. Her expertise includes leading technology- and software-intensive projects, executive coaching, building and leading cross-functional teams, and program management for large, complex engagements. Ms. Ziemski has more than 20 years of experience in project management, including experience in product development, account management, business process reengineering, organizational development, technology deployment, project management training, mentoring, and team building. Ms. Ziemski has managed complex projects in the telecommunications, professional services, and manufacturing industries.

Ms. Ziemski's consulting experience includes engagements with multiple agencies within the federal government, as well as industry engagements with AT&T, Toyota Financial Services, Boeing, Toyota Motor Sales, various not-for-profit employment groups, SABRE Technologies, and Dow Jones. Client services included maturity assessments, project launches, troubled project recovery, and project portfolio management processes. Ms. Ziemski's focus on communications, leadership, conflict resolution, and negotiations has been instrumental in her ability to deliver top-of-class results both in her corporate career with AT&T and as an independent consultant.

Ms. Ziemski earned a B.S. in information technologies management from American Intercontinental University and is a qualified administrator of the Myers-Briggs Type Indicator®.

Table of Contents

Preface

The Business Analysis Essential Library is a series of books that each cover a separate and distinct area of business analysis. The business analyst ensures that there is a strong business focus for the projects that emerge as a result of the fierce, competitive nature and rapid rate of change of business today. Within both private industry and government agencies, the business analyst is becoming the central figure in leading major change initiatives. This library is designed to explain the emerging role of the business analyst and present contemporary business analysis practices (the what), supported by practical tools and techniques to enable the application of the practices (the how).

Current books in the series are:

- *Professionalizing Business Analysis: Breaking the Cycle of Challenged Projects*

- *The Business Analyst as Strategist: Translating Business Strategies into Valuable Solutions*

- *Unearthing Business Requirements: Elicitation Tools and Techniques*

- *Getting it Right: Business Requirement Analysis Tools and Techniques*

- *The Art and Power of Facilitation: Running Powerful Meetings*

+ *From Analyst to Leader: Elevating the Role of the Business Analyst*

Check the Management Concepts website, www.managementconcepts.com/pubs, for updates to this series.

About This Book

The goal of this book is to arm business analysts with the principles, knowledge, practices, and tools they need to assume leadership roles in their organizations. Although the business analyst is primarily responsible for writing and managing requirements specifications and communicating them to stakeholders, the incidence of business analysts serving as internal business and technology consultants is rapidly emerging. A 2006 custom research study conducted for Compuware® by Evans Data Corporation and the Requirements Networking Group revealed that business analysts spend no less than 15.3 percent of their time defining the big picture, business objectives, and measures of success.[1] Therefore, while you acquire and sustain your business analysis knowledge and skills, it's a good idea to consider your leadership prowess as well.

---

1 Compuware® Corporation, in association with Evans Data Corporation and the
   Requirements Networking Group, *The New Business Analyst: A Strategic Role in the
   Enterprise*, November 2006, http://www.compuware.com/ (accessed July 2007).

Part I

Leadership in a Project Environment

The first part of this book describes the challenging leadership role that lies ahead for business analysts who have the passion and ambition to become strategic leaders of change for their organizations.

In Chapter 1 we present the concept of twenty-first century leadership in a project environment. We describe the relationship between project leadership and the traditional concept of leadership in a business enterprise. In addition, we discuss the power of the project leadership team, of which the business analyst is a central figure.

In Chapter 2 we present the unique challenges for the business analyst to transition from a support role to the role of a key leader serving as change agent, visionary, and credible guide.

In Chapter 3 we discuss the business analyst's role as it changes throughout the business solution life cycle.

+ The ability to elicit extraordinary performance from ordinary people

+ The capacity to integrate the goals of the organization with the aspirations of the people through a shared vision and committed action

+ The ability to motivate people to work toward a common goal

While there are no gauges by which we can effectively measure the value of leadership, leadership is often the factor that makes one team more effective than another. Leaders are often held accountable for team successes and failures. When a team succeeds, we often remark about keen leadership abilities; when a team fails, the leader is likely to receive the blame.

Leadership is people-centered. It always involves actions by a leader (influencer) to affect (influence) the behavior of a follower or followers in a specific situation or activity. Three contributing factors must be present for true leadership to take place: inborn characteristics, learned skills, and the right situation. We may not be able to do much to shape our inborn leadership characteristics, but we certainly can create the appropriate learning opportunities and try to influence our current situation and environment.

Twenty-First Century Leadership

In decades gone by, business leadership was considered the province of just a few people who controlled the organization. In today's rapidly changing business environment, however, organizations rely on a remarkable array of leaders who operate at varying levels of the enterprise. Twenty-first century leadership looks very different from that of previous centuries for several reasons: the economic environment is more volatile than ever before, there is a strong need for more leadership at differing levels of the organization, and lifelong

+ The ability to elicit extraordinary performance from ordinary people

+ The capacity to integrate the goals of the organization with the aspirations of the people through a shared vision and committed action

+ The ability to motivate people to work toward a common goal

While there are no gauges by which we can effectively measure the value of leadership, leadership is often the factor that makes one team more effective than another. Leaders are often held accountable for team successes and failures. When a team succeeds, we often remark about keen leadership abilities; when a team fails, the leader is likely to receive the blame.

Leadership is people-centered. It always involves actions by a leader (influencer) to affect (influence) the behavior of a follower or followers in a specific situation or activity. Three contributing factors must be present for true leadership to take place: inborn characteristics, learned skills, and the right situation. We may not be able to do much to shape our inborn leadership characteristics, but we certainly can create the appropriate learning opportunities and try to influence our current situation and environment.

Twenty-First Century Leadership

In decades gone by, business leadership was considered the province of just a few people who controlled the organization. In today's rapidly changing business environment, however, organizations rely on a remarkable array of leaders who operate at varying levels of the enterprise. Twenty-first century leadership looks very different from that of previous centuries for several reasons: the economic environment is more volatile than ever before, there is a strong need for more leadership at differing levels of the organization, and lifelong

Chapter 1

Project Leadership

In This Chapter:

- Twenty-First Century Leadership
- Twenty-First Century Projects
- Management versus Leadership
- Combining Disciplines Leads to Success
- The Power of the Project Leadership Team
- The New Project Leader
- The Core Project Team

> Leadership is a potent combination of strategy and character.
> But if you must be without one, be without strategy.
> Gen. H. Norman Schwarzkopf

Leadership is one of those concepts that is recognizable when you observe it in action but is otherwise somewhat difficult to define. Books about leadership abound, each describing the concept in a different way. Leadership can be defined as:

- The art of persuading or influencing other people to set aside their individual concerns and to pursue a common goal that is important for the welfare of the group

**Part I**

Leadership in a Project Environment

*T*he first part of this book describes the challenging leadership role that lies ahead for business analysts who have the passion and ambition to become strategic leaders of change for their organizations.

In Chapter 1 we present the concept of twenty-first century leadership in a project environment. We describe the relationship between project leadership and the traditional concept of leadership in a business enterprise. In addition, we discuss the power of the project leadership team, of which the business analyst is a central figure.

In Chapter 2 we present the unique challenges for the business analyst to transition from a support role to the role of a key leader serving as change agent, visionary, and credible guide.

In Chapter 3 we discuss the business analyst's role as it changes throughout the business solution life cycle.

learning is at the heart of professional success. The most valuable employees will no longer stay in narrow functional areas but will likely work broadly across the enterprise.

As we transition from the traditional stovepipe, function-centric structures to the project-centric workplace, we are seeing the emergence of project management and business analysis as critical business practices. Work has been transformed from multiple workers performing a single task to teams that perform multiple activities on multiple projects, and twenty-first century projects are larger, more strategic, and more complex than ever before.

Twenty-First Century Projects

Virtually all organizations of any size are investing in large-scale transformations of one kind or another. Contemporary projects are about adding value to the organization with breakthrough ideas, optimizing business processes, and using information technology (IT) as a competitive advantage. These initiatives are often spawned by mergers or acquisitions, new strategies, global competition, or the emergence of new technologies. Other initiatives are launched to implement new or reengineered business systems aimed at driving waste out of business operations.

Most of these changes are accompanied by organizational restructuring, new partnerships, cultural transformation, downsizing or right-sizing, and the development of enabling IT systems. Others involve implementing new lines of business and new ways of doing business (e.g., e-business).

In addition to these business-driven changes, IT organizations are transforming themselves, striving to become more service-oriented and better aligned with the business. In the twenty-first century, project teams no longer deal with IT projects in isolation but within the overarching process of business transformation. The reach of change affects all areas of the organization and beyond—to customers, suppliers, and business partners—making the complexity of projects considerable.

Rather than undertaking only a small number of projects, today's organizations are engaged in virtually hundreds of ongoing projects of varying sizes, durations, and levels of complexity. Business strategy is largely achieved through projects. Projects are essential to the growth and survival of organizations. They create value in the form of new products and services as a response to changes in the business environment, competition, and the marketplace.

To reap the rewards of significant, large-scale business transformation initiatives designed not only to keep organizations in the game but also to make them major players, we must be able to manage complex business transformation projects effectively. Huge cost and schedule overruns, however, have been commonplace in the past. According to leading research companies such as The Standish Group International, Inc., the Software Engineering Institute at Carnegie Mellon University, Gartner, Forrester Research, and Meta Group, vastly inadequate business transformation and information technology project performance has been the order of the day. The actual numbers are at best disappointing, if not unacceptable:[1]

- About $80 to $145 billion per year is spent on failed and canceled projects.

- As a result of rework, 25 to 40 percent of all spending on projects is wasted.

- Fifty percent of new business solutions are rolled back out of production.

- Forty percent of problems are found by end users.

- Poorly defined applications have led to persistent miscommunication between business and IT that largely contributes to a 66 percent project failure rate for these applications, costing U.S. businesses at least $30 billion every year.

+ An estimated 60 to 80 percent of project failures can be attributed directly to poor requirements gathering, analysis, and management.

+ Nearly two-thirds of all IT projects fail or run into trouble.

These dismal statistics and the increased importance of projects in executing business strategies have advanced the value and criticality of project leaders, including project managers, business analysts, technologists, and business visionaries. It is important to recognize the differences between traditional project management and project leadership in this context.

Management versus Leadership

Management competency involves establishing and executing a set of processes that keep a complicated system operating efficiently. Key aspects of management involve planning, budgeting, organizing, staffing, controlling, and problem solving. Some say management is about keeping bureaucracies functioning.

Leadership is a different set of processes, those that create a new organization and change it when the business environment shifts significantly. Leadership involves establishing direction and aligning, motivating, and inspiring people to produce change. The irony is that as new or changed organizations emerge, succeed, and grow through leadership and entrepreneurship, managerial processes need to be put into place to cope with the growth and control the system. As the organization succeeds and managerial processes are put in place, arrogance tends to surface and a strong culture that is resistant to change develops.[2]

Although there are similarities in the roles of manager, leader, and project leader, there are subtle differences as well. Table 1-1 shows the distinctions between these roles to help you understand the differences as you hone your project leadership competency.

Table 1-1—Comparing Leadership Roles

Objective	Manager	Leader	Project Leader
Define what must be done	Planning and budgeting • Short timeframe • Detail-oriented • Eliminating risk	Establishing direction • Long timeframe • Big picture • Calculated risk	Establishing project goals and objectives • Project mission and direction • Alignment with strategy
Create networks of people and relationships	Organizing and staffing • Specialization • Getting the right people • Compliance	Aligning people • Integration • Aligning the organization • Gaining commitment	Aligning core team and stakeholders • Integration • Expectations • Political mastery • Gaining commitment
Ensure the job gets done	Controlling and problem solving • Containment • Control • Predictability	Motivating and inspiring • Empowerment • Expansion • Energizing	Team building and coaching • High performance • Developing trust • Removing barriers

Organizations in the past have focused on *management* and virtually excluded the vital role of *leadership* in projects. The project manager focused heavily on planning, budgeting, organizing, staffing, monitoring, and controlling. All project team members report to the project manager regarding project work assigned to them. Figure 1-1 depicts a traditional project team configuration.

Twenty-first century project teams are required to focus less on management and control, and focus more on leadership, collaboration, and forming multi-disciplinary teams to succeed.

Combining Disciplines Leads to Success

In the last four decades, we have discovered the full power and potential of using information technology effectively. Superior business solutions supported by enabling technology can bring about a

Figure 1-1—Traditional Project Team Configuration

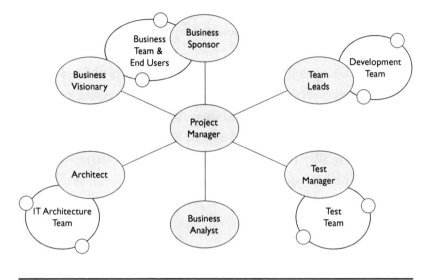

significant competitive advantage. In the absence of business-focused project leaders, we often focused on the technology, asked the senior engineer to serve as the project manager, and virtually overlooked the critical role of the business analyst.

All too often, expertise in the technical area of the project was the sole criterion for a project leadership position. Time and again, projects experienced difficulties—not from lack of technical expertise, but from an inability to understand the business need and the strong cultural influences, manage the politics, secure the appropriate resources, and build high-performing project teams. There was often a low tolerance for technical failure and a high tolerance for rework, cost overruns, and schedule delays.

As projects become larger and more cross-functional, global, and complex, organizations are realizing that business analysis and project management leadership skills are indispensable. In the last two decades, the focus of project management has been on quantitative skills like cost management, schedule management, quality control, scope management, and configuration management. Technically competent engineers have made the professional transition to the discipline of project management as a by-product of their technical mastery.

These project managers tend to focus on the tools and techniques used to plan projects, estimate costs and resource requirements, issue requests for proposals, award contracts, and monitor and control issues and risks—the technical side of project management. Often these persons play multiple leadership roles on projects—the role of technical lead, requirements engineer, lead architect, and project manager. Inevitably, after the initial planning activities are complete, the technical activities tend to win most of the project manager's attention.

It is now becoming clear that the technical project management knowledge areas are necessary but not sufficient to successfully manage the large, enterprise-wide, complex, mission-critical projects that are the norm today. Indeed, it takes a business-focused leadership team with diverse skills and perspectives to pull it off. Combining the business analysis and project management disciplines to corral the best business and technical minds holds great potential. Investing in project leaders and high-performing project teams reaps rewards in terms of reduced cost, lower risk, and faster time to project delivery.

The Power of the Project Leadership Team

Organizations use projects to add value to their products and services to better serve their clients and compete in the marketplace. To realize their goals, organizations tap into the talents and competencies of project leadership teams consisting of the business analyst, the project manager, technologists, and business visionaries.

As discussed in detail in another volume in this series, *The Business Analyst as Strategist: Translating Business Strategies into Valuable Solutions*, project-driven organizations develop a portfolio of projects. Executives spend a great deal of time identifying which projects offer the greatest rewards with minimal risks. However, to make good project investment decisions, executives are discovering the need for business analysis to provide solid information backing their decisions.

The business analyst provides the processes, tools, and information that enable executives to develop a portfolio of valuable projects. The business analyst then transitions to focus on project execution to meet business needs and maximize the organization's return on project investment.

It is not enough for executive teams to just select the right mix of projects to achieve their strategic imperatives. Executive teams must also establish the organizational capabilities to deliver. Project teams must be capable of contributing to the organization's success. For optimal project execution, several elements are essential:

- Appropriate management support and decision-making at key control gates

- Effective and targeted business analysis, systems engineering, and project management processes, tools, and techniques

- Technical infrastructure and software applications that are tightly aligned with the business

- High-performing teams

It is especially important for executives to develop exceptional project managers and business analysts so they can transition into effective project leaders. Figure 1-2, the Business Analyst and Project Management Leadership Model, depicts the transition from capable individual to world-class project leader. The performance of the business analyst is more critical than ever to keep the project team focused on the business benefits sought through project outcomes.

Figure 1-2—Business Analyst and Project Management Leadership Model

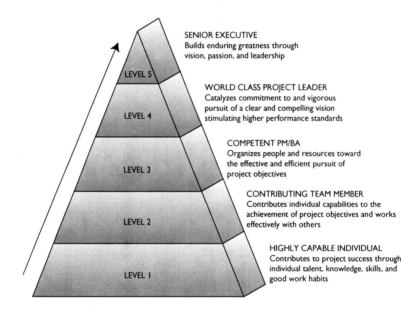

SENIOR EXECUTIVE
Builds enduring greatness through vision, passion, and leadership

WORLD CLASS PROJECT LEADER
Catalyzes commitment to and vigorous pursuit of a clear and compelling vision stimulating higher performance standards

COMPETENT PM/BA
Organizes people and resources toward the effective and efficient pursuit of project objectives

CONTRIBUTING TEAM MEMBER
Contributes individual capabilities to the achievement of project objectives and works effectively with others

HIGHLY CAPABLE INDIVIDUAL
Contributes to project success through individual talent, knowledge, skills, and good work habits

With so much riding on successful projects, the *business analyst* is emerging to fill the information gap between strategy and execution, the *project manager* has risen to the role of strategic implementer, and *cross-functional project teams* have become management's strategic tool to convert strategy to action.

When the project manager and business analyst form a strong partnership with the business and technology teams, they will begin to reap the maximum value of both disciplines. As the business analysis and project management disciplines mature into strategic business practices, so must our project leaders evolve into strategic leaders of change.

The New Project Leader

As programs and projects are launched to realize critical strategic goals, leaders of strategic initiatives should be looked upon as the executive officer team of a small enterprise. Just as a business leader must be multiskilled and strategically focused, a project leader must possess a broad range of knowledge and experience, including competence in several distinct areas—general management, project management, business analysis, the application area (the domain), leadership, and business/technology optimization. Refer to Figure 1-3 for a view of project leadership competency areas and Table 1-2 for a summary of knowledge and skill requirements.

Figure 1-3—Project Leader Competency Groups

Clearly, a well-formed team of experts is equipped to provide the requisite knowledge and skills better than a single individual. In the twenty-first century, small-but-mighty, high-performing teams of experts are a vital strategic asset.

Table 1-2—Project Leader Knowledge and Skill Requirements

General Management Knowledge and Practice	Project Management Knowledge and Practice	Application Area Knowledge and Practice	Leadership Knowledge and Skills	Business Analysis Knowledge and Practice
• Business areas (e.g., marketing, finance) • Administrative policies, procedures, business rules • Regulatory requirements • Strategic planning, goal setting	• Integration management • Scope management • Time management • Cost management • Communications management • Quality management • Procurement management • Human resource management • Risk management • Program management • Portfolio management	• Information technology • Technical areas of the project • Systems engineering • Software engineering • Domain knowledge • Products • Markets	• People management • Team building • Organizational behavior • Political maneuvering • Change management • Strategic alignment • Conflict management • Negotiating • Communications	• Business opportunity identification • Alternative solution analysis • Cost versus benefit analysis • Requirements planning, management, elicitation, analysis, specification, communication • Solution assessment and validation • Consulting skills

The Core Project Team

It is now becoming clear that successful projects are more about collaboration and leadership as opposed to command and control. In the twenty-first century, the project team structure is transitioning to one of team leadership versus project management. Consider the core project team configuration represented in Figure 1-4. Using this approach, the core team is small, multi-disciplined, dedicated to the project full-time, and co-located. The core team forms sub-teams and brings in subject matter experts when needed.

Figure 1-4—Core Project Team Configuration

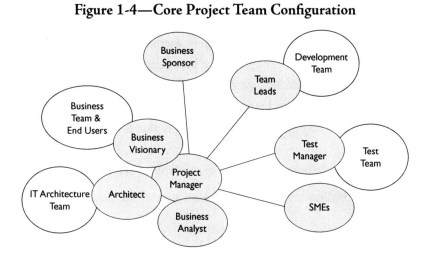

This core team shares the leadership of the project, each person taking the lead when his or her expertise is needed. Shared leadership does not mean there is no accountability. The project manager is still responsible for ensuring that the business solution is delivered on time, on budget, and with the full scope promised. The business analyst is responsible for ensuring that the project team fully understands the business need and the benefits expected from the new solution, and for validating that the solution meets the requirements and will deliver the expected business benefits. The architect ensures that the solution is designed and developed according to specifications. The business visionary continues to keep the team focused on the big picture, the strategic goal that will be advanced by the new solution; brings in the appropriate business experts when needed; and helps prepare the organization to operate in a new way once the business solution is deployed.

Whereas in the past project teams revolved around the project manager as their leader, the very nature of project team leadership is changing. The team leadership changes subtly based on the needs of the project. The project manager still leads the project management activities. During requirements elicitation, the business analyst takes the lead and the other core team members slide into more of a support role. As the project moves into solution design and development, the technical architect or developer often assumes the lead role. All core leadership team members support each other, and they get out of the way when their expertise is not the critical element needed.

In the next chapter, we will explore the role of the business analyst as project leader in more detail.

Endnotes

1. For more information on the research institutions mentioned in this chapter, please visit the following websites: Standish Group International, Inc. (http://www.standishgroup.com/), the Software Engineering Institute at Carnegie Mellon University (http://www.sei.cmu.edu/), Gartner and Meta Group research services (http://www.gartner.com/it/products/research/research_services.jsp), and Forrester Research (http://www.forrester.com/rb/research).

2. John P. Kotter. *Leading Change*, 1996. Boston: Harvard Business School Press.

Chapter 2

The Business Analyst as Project Leader

In This Chapter:

- The Business Analyst as Change Agent
- The Business Analyst as Visionary
- The Business Analyst as Credible Leader

The business analyst, serving as one of several project leaders, closes the gap on areas that have historically been woefully overlooked in business transformation and innovation projects. Some of the areas that the business analyst directs more attention to include:

- Integrating strategic planning with planning for the information systems and technology directions

- Defining business problems and identifying new business opportunities to achieve the strategic vision

- Understanding the business need and impacts of the proposed solution on all areas of business operations

- Maintaining a fierce focus on the value the project is expected to bring to the enterprise

- Using an integrated set of analysis and modeling techniques to make the as-is and to-be business environments visible for all to see, understand, and validate

+ Translating the business objectives into business requirements using powerful modeling tools

+ Validating that the new solution meets the business need

+ Managing the benefits expected from the new solution

Serving as a key project leader with a constant focus on adding value to the business, the business analyst becomes a powerful change agent.

The Business Analyst as Change Agent

According to John P. Kotter, "The rate of change is not going to slow down anytime soon. If anything, competition in most industries will probably speed up even more in the next few decades."[1] Kotter goes on to say that as the rate of change increases, the willingness and ability of knowledge workers to acquire new knowledge and skills become central to career success for individuals, as well as to the economic success of organizations. Professionals must develop the capacity to handle a complex and changing business environment. Along the way, they grow to become unusually competent in advancing organizational transformation. *They learn to be leaders.*

Without a doubt, the level of large-scale organizational change has grown exponentially over the past two decades. Although some predict that the amount of change in terms of reengineering, mergers and acquisitions, restructuring, downsizing, quality improvement efforts, and cultural transformation projects will soon diminish, all indications are that change is here to stay. Powerful economic and social forces are at work to drive major organizational change initiatives, including technological advances, global economic integration, maturation of markets in developed countries, emerging markets in the developing countries, and the changing political landscape.[2]

Culture in an organization is typically described as "the way we do things around here." Changing the way we select projects, develop and manage requirements, and manage projects while focusing on business value is often a significant change for organizations. Many organizational cultures believe in piling project requests, accompanied by sparse requirements, onto the information technology (IT) group and then wondering why IT cannot seem to deliver.

Conversely, mature organizations devote a significant amount of time and energy to conducting business analysis prior to selecting and prioritizing projects (as discussed in another volume in this series, *The Business Analyst as Strategist: Translating Business Strategies into Valuable Solutions*) and then develop and manage requirements (as discussed in two other volumes in this series, *Unearthing Business Requirements: Elicitation Tools and Techniques* and *Getting it Right: Business Requirement Analysis Tools and Techniques*). This new approach involves a significant cultural shift for most organizations.

Rita Hadden provides us with some insight into the enormity of the effort it takes to truly change the way we do projects.[3] To achieve culture change, you must have a management plan to deal with the technical complexity of the change and a leadership plan to address the human aspects of the change. According to Hadden, successful culture change requires at a minimum the following elements:[4]

+ A compelling vision and call to action

+ Credible knowledge and skills to guide the change

+ A reward system aligned with the change

+ Adequate resources to implement the change

+ A detailed plan and schedule

Hadden goes on to say that change agents need to understand the concerns and motivations of the people they hope to influence. They must clearly define the desired outcomes for the change and how to measure progress, assess the organization's readiness for change, and develop plans to minimize the barriers to success.[5]

One of the critical roles of the business analyst (and the entire project leadership team) is to effect change—to become a leader of change. Competitive pressures are forcing organizations to reassess their fundamental structures and operations. The amount of change today is formidable. While some react to change with anger, confusion, and dismay, it falls upon the project manager and business analyst to lead the transformations required by most organizations.

The role of the business analyst as change agent, effecting change through projects, takes on many forms:

+ Fostering the concept that projects are business problems, solved by teams of people using technology as a strategic tool

+ Working as a strategic implementer of change, focusing on the business benefits expected from the project to achieve strategies

+ Changing the way the business interacts with the technical team, often significantly increasing the amount of business resources/expertise dedicated to projects

+ Encouraging the technical team members to work collaboratively with the business representatives

+ Building high-performing project teams that focus more on the business value of the project than on the new technology

+ Preparing the organization to accept new business solutions and to operate them efficiently

+ Measuring the actual benefits new business solutions bring to the organization

Most of these changes dramatically affect the organizational culture and the way we manage projects.

The Business Analyst as Visionary

A common vision is essential to bring about significant change. A clear vision helps to direct, align, and inspire actions. Without a clear vision, a lofty transformation project can be reduced to a list of inconsequential projects that sap energy and drain valuable resources. Most importantly, a clear vision guides decision making so that every decision that needs to be made is not subjected to unneeded debate and conflict. Yet, we continue to underestimate the power of vision.

Whether implementing professional business analysis practices or a major new business solution, the business analyst needs to articulate a clear vision and then involve the many stakeholders in the change initiative as early as possible. Executives and middle managers are essential allies in bringing about change of any magnitude. They all must deliver a consistent message about the need for the change. Select the most credible and influential members of your organization, seek their advice and counsel, and have them become the *voice of change*. The greater the number of influential managers, executives, and technical/business experts articulating the same vision, the better chance you have of being successful.

The Business Analyst as Credible Leader

The business analyst, when acting as a change agent, needs to develop and sustain a high level of credibility. Credible business professionals are sought out by all organizations. People want to be associated with them. They are thought of as being trustworthy, reliable, and sincere. The business analyst can develop his or her credibility to bring about organizational change by becoming proficient at these critical skills:

+ Practicing business outcome thinking

+ Conceptualizing and thinking creatively

+ Acquiring interpersonal skills

- Valuing ethics and integrity

- Using robust communication techniques to effectively keep all stakeholders informed

- Empowering team members and building high-performing teams

- Setting direction and providing vision

- Listening effectively and encouraging new ideas

- Seeking responsibility and accepting accountability

- Focusing and motivating a group to achieve what is important

- Capitalizing on the contributions of various team members

- Managing complexity dimensions to reduce project risks

- Welcoming changes that promote the integrity of the solution/product

A credible leader is one others can trust and believe in. Above all, a business analyst must strive to be a credible source of information. Credibility is composed of both trustworthiness and expertise. Colleagues often judge credibility on subjective factors, too, such as enthusiasm and even physical appearance. But at the end of the day, ethics and integrity are the cornerstones of credibility.

In Part II we discuss the critical skills the business analyst needs to become a credible leader in more detail. But first, in the next chapter we outline the business analyst's role throughout the project life cycle.

Endnotes

1. John P. Kotter. *Leading Change*, 1996. Boston: Harvard Business School Press.

2. Ibid.

3. Rita Chao Hadden. *Leading Culture Change in Your Software Organization: Delivering Results Early*, 2003. Vienna, VA: Management Concepts, Inc.

4. Ibid.

5. Ibid.

Chapter 3

The Business Analyst's Leadership Role throughout the Business Solution Life Cycle

In This Chapter:

- The Business Analyst's Role in Strategic Planning and Enterprise Analysis

- The Business Analyst's Role in Requirements and Design

- The Business Analyst's Role in Construction and Testing

- The Business Analyst's Role in Solution Delivery

- The Business Analyst's Role in Operations and Maintenance

Throughout the Business Analysis Essential Library, we have used the business solution life cycle (BSLC) model as a framework for our discussions about the role of the business analyst. This model, shown in Figure 3-1, depicts the major deliverables produced, as well as the skills and techniques employed by the business analyst during each project phase. The business analyst partners and collaborates with other key project leaders, the project manager, business representatives, and technical leads during all phases of the BSLC.

Figure 3-1—The Business Solution Life Cycle

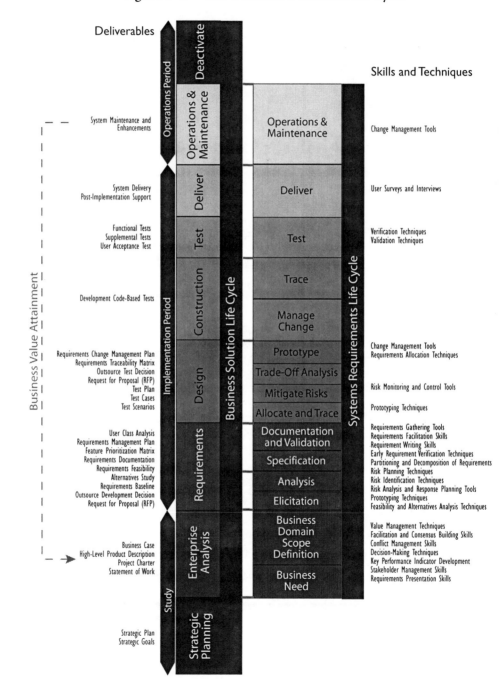

The Business Analyst's Role in Strategic Planning and Enterprise Analysis

The business analyst is largely responsible for providing information, processes, and tools, as well as for facilitating an organizational focus on strategy execution through projects. During the strategic planning and enterprise analysis phases, the business analyst conducts competitive analysis and benchmark studies, identifies potential solutions to business problems, conducts feasibility studies to determine the optimum solution, and prepares the business case for the proposed new initiative to arm the executive team with the information it needs to make quality project investment decisions. A high-quality decision is one that is likely to attain the goals of the organization, is well reasoned, and is consistent with available information and with organizational goals and objectives.

The foremost business analysis leadership skills needed during these phases include:

Soft Skills and Techniques

+ Facilitation and consensus building

+ Conflict management

+ Consensus decision-making

+ Customer management

+ Communications

+ Stakeholder management

+ Management of politics and power

Technical Skills and Techniques

+ Business modeling

+ Competitive analysis

+ Benchmarking

+ Feasibility analysis

+ Cost versus benefit analysis

+ Business case development

+ Business metrics and measurement development

+ Benefits management

+ Product sizing

Refer to another volume in this series, *The Business Analyst as Strategist: Translating Business Strategies into Valuable Solutions,* for a detailed description of the activities and deliverables produced and the role of the business analyst during the strategic planning and enterprise analysis project phases.

The Business Analyst's Role in Requirements and Design

During the requirements and design phases, the business analyst conducts requirements elicitation, analysis, specification, documentation, validation, and change management activities. At the same time, the business analyst works with the solution designers to make the necessary tradeoffs to deliver the solution on time and with the required scope of features and functions.

The business analysis leadership skills needed during these phases include:

Soft Skills and Techniques

+ Problem solving

- Team building

- Communication

- Conflict management

- Consensus decision-making

- Negotiations

- Customer relationship management

- Managing politics and stakeholders

- Organizational change management

- Facilitation skills

- Stakeholder management

Technical Skills and Techniques

- Requirements engineering

- Requirements elicitation

- Requirements validation and verification

- Requirements partitioning and decomposition

- Requirements allocation

- Requirements change management

- Requirements specification and documentation

- Requirements risk planning and monitoring

- Requirements baseline management

- Alternative solution identification and analysis

- Prototyping techniques

- Requirements understanding modeling

- Proof of concept

- Scope decomposition and progressive elaboration

- Business writing

- Issue resolution

- Problem solving

Refer to two other volumes in this series, *Unearthing Business Requirements: Elicitation Tools and Techniques* and *Getting it Right: Business Requirement Analysis Tools and Techniques*, for a detailed description of the activities and deliverables produced during the requirements and design project phases.

The Business Analyst's Role in Construction and Testing

During the construction and testing phases, the business analyst continually validates the requirements and early system prototypes and builds end-user procedures, education, documentation, and transition plans.

The business analysis leadership skills needed during these phases include:

Soft Skills and Techniques

- Problem solving

- Team building

- Communication

- Conflict management

- Consensus decision-making

- Negotiations

- Customer relationship management (managing politics and stakeholders)

- Organizational change management

Technical Skills and Techniques

- Requirements change management

- Requirements traceability (to physical components)

- Business writing

- Verification and validation

- Development and implementation of policies, procedures, business rules, and training manuals

The Business Analyst's Role in Solution Delivery

The business analyst assumes the lead role during solution delivery to ensure that the implementation plans are well communicated and accepted by the business groups undergoing change. During deployment, the business analyst conducts training, facilitates the implementation of business procedures and policies, and works to ensure that the solution is delivering the expected business value.

The foremost business analysis leadership skills needed during these phases include:

Soft Skills and Techniques

- Organizational change planning and management

- Problem solving

- Communication

- Conflict management

- Consensus decision-making

- Negotiations

- Customer relationship management (managing politics and stakeholders)

- Organizational change management

- Mentoring and coaching

Technical Skills and Techniques

- Training

- Timely issue resolution

- Prioritization

- Problem solving

- Root cause analysis

- Corrective actions

- Quality management

- Identification and implementation of procedural work-arounds

- Solution value measurement

The Business Analyst's Role in Operations and Maintenance

During the operations and maintenance phase, the business analyst identifies, prioritizes and implements enhancements to the solution to continue to add value to the business. The business analyst continually monitors the performance of the solution, ensures that defects that arise are corrected, and reports on actual benefits of the solution to the person(s) who sponsored the project and are accountable for the business benefits. Finally, the business analyst determines when the solution is no longer adding the required value to the organization and recommends deactivation and replacement.

The most important leadership skills needed during these phases include:

Soft Skills and Techniques

+ Problem solving

+ Communication

+ Customer relationship management (managing politics and stakeholders)

+ Organizational change management

+ Mentoring and coaching

Technical Skills and Techniques

+ Measurement analysis

+ Metric analysis

+ Cost/benefit analysis

+ Solution value measurement

+ Qualitative and quantitative analysis

+ Root cause analysis

+ Corrective actions

+ Identification and implementation of procedural work-arounds

So there you have it—a broad overview of the business analyst's leadership role throughout the BSLC. Read on to examine key aspects of the leadership acumen needed and recommendations for a path from business analysis to business leadership.

Part II
Business Analyst as Project Leader

*I*n this part of the book, we discuss some of the critical knowledge and skills needed by the business analyst in his or her role as one of the central project leaders.

In Chapter 4, we discuss team leadership, team development, and the role of the business analyst in building a high-performing requirements team and in helping the project manager build the project team. One of the contributing authors, Kimi Ziemski, explains the subtleties of working with teams during their development phases.

In Chapter 5, Ms. Ziemski explains why it is important for the business analyst to become a powerful communicator. She discusses communication building blocks and the value of active listening.

In Chapter 6, contributing author Richard Vander Horst shares his insights on how the business analyst and other project team leaders manage customer relationships, traversing the power struggles and political minefields that are ever-present on complex, large-scale change initiatives.

Chapter 4

The Business Analyst as Team Leader

In This Chapter:

- The Power of Teams

- Team Development through Stages

- Traversing the Team Development Stages

- Team Leadership Roles through Stages

- Best Team-Building Practices for the Business Analyst

- Quick Team Assessment

The need for effective team leadership cannot be overlooked. Technology, techniques, and tools don't cause projects to fail. Projects fail because of people. Team leadership is different from traditional management, and teams are different from operational work groups. As we discussed in Part I, when leading high-performing teams, it is no longer about command and control; it is more about collaboration, consensus, and leadership.

As discussed in *The Art and Power of Facilitation: Running Powerful Meetings,* another volume in this series, team leaders must have an understanding of how teams work and the dynamics of team development. Team leaders develop specialized skills that are used to build and maintain high-performing teams. Traditional managers and technical leads cannot necessarily become effective team leaders without the appropriate mindset, training, and coaching.

In 1995 *Fortune* magazine's Thomas Stewart predicted that project management would be the profession of choice in the coming decade. He cited current trends toward global initiatives, virtual teams, mergers and acquisitions, downsizing and reengineering, and alliances and partnerships—all linking companies in new ways.[1] The Project Management Institute has been alerting us for years that cross-cultural training and awareness, interpersonal skills, and language facility will increasingly grow to be conditions for professional success as a project manager. To manage twenty-first century projects, these characteristics are not just nice to have; they are vital.

> "A small group of thoughtful people could change the world. Indeed, it's the only thing that ever has."
> Margaret Mead, American cultural anthropologist

Teams are a critical asset used to improve performance in all kinds of organizations. Yet today's business leaders consistently overlook opportunities to exploit their potential, confusing teams with teamwork, empowerment, or participative management.[2] We cannot meet the twenty-first century challenges—from business transformation to innovation to global competition—without high-performing teams.

The Power of Teams

Examples of high-performing teams are all around us: U.S. Navy SEALs, tiger teams established to solve a difficult problem, paramedic teams, firefighter teams, heart transplant teams, and professional sports teams, just to name a few. These teams demonstrate their accomplishments, insights, and enthusiasm daily and are a persuasive testament to the power of teams.

Yet the business project environment, especially the IT project environment, has been slow to capitalize on the power of teams. It is imperative that senior business analysts understand how to unleash this power. Business success stories based on the strategic use of teams for new product development abound. For example, 3M relies on new product development teams for its success. These teams are cross-functional, collaborative, autonomous, and self-organizing. The teams deal well with ambiguity, accept change, take initiative, and assume risks. 3M has established the goal of generating half of each year's revenues from the previous five years' innovations, and its use of teams is critical to meeting that goal.[3]

Another success story is Toyota, which continues to boast the fastest product development times in the automotive industry, is a consistent leader in quality, has a large variety of products designed by a lean engineering staff, and has consistently grown its U.S. market share. Teams at Toyota are led by a chief engineer who is expected to understand the market and whose primary job is vehicle system design. The chief engineer is responsible for vehicle development, similar to a product champion at 3M.[4]

Economists have been warning us for years that success in a global marketplace is contingent upon our capability to produce products on a tight schedule to meet growing demands in emerging markets. The same is true of projects to improve business performance: It's not enough to deliver projects on time and within budget and scope; it is now necessary to deliver *value* to the organization faster, cheaper, and better. In the business world, it's important to learn how to form and develop high-performing project teams that can deliver project outcomes quickly.

For the business analyst who is struggling to understand how to build high-performing teams, a must-read is *The Wisdom of Teams* by Jon Katzenbach and Douglas Smith.[5] The authors talked with hundreds of people on more than 50 different teams in 30 companies to discover what differentiates various levels of team performance, where and how teams work best, and how to enhance team effectiveness. Among their findings are elements of both common and uncommon sense:

- A commitment to performance goals and common purpose is more important to team success than team building.

- Opportunities for teams exist in all parts of the organization.

- Formal hierarchy is actually good for teams, and vice versa.

- Successful team leaders do not fit an ideal profile and are not necessarily the most senior people on the team.

- Real teams are the most common characteristic of successful change efforts at all levels.

- Top management teams are often difficult to sustain.

- Despite the increased number of teams, team performance potential is largely unrecognized and underutilized.

- Adjourning teams can be just as important to manage as forming teams.

- Teams produce a unique blend of performance and personal learning results.

Wisdom lies in recognizing a team's unique potential to deliver results. Project leaders strive to understand the many benefits of teams and learn how to optimize team performance by developing individual members, fostering team cohesiveness, and awarding team results. Katzenbach and Smith argue that teams are the primary building blocks of strong company performance. Business analysts at all levels cannot afford to ignore the power of teams to meet the competitive challenges of the twenty-first century.[6]

Team Development through Stages

As a member of the project leadership team, the business analyst is partially responsible for helping to build a high-performing team, and fully responsible for building a high-performing requirements definition team. To successfully develop such a team, it is helpful to understand the key stages of team development. Using the classic team development model from Bruce Tuckman as a guide, contributing author Kimi Ziemski discusses the team development issues that could present challenges to team effectiveness. The Tuckman model has become an accepted paradigm of how teams develop.

Tuckman outlines the five stages of team development: forming, storming, norming, performing and adjourning.[7] As the team transitions from one stage to another, the needs of the team and its individual members vary. A successful team leader knows which stage the team is in, and skillfully manages transitions between the different stages. Figure 4-1 depicts the typical stages of team development. The following sections outline the five stages of team development in detail. We then discuss the team leadership roles project team leaders need during each stage.

Figure 4-1—Stages of Team Development

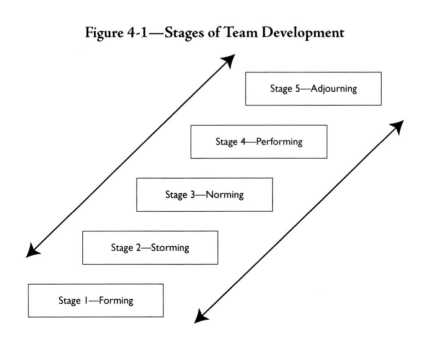

Forming Stage

The forming stage involves the introduction of team members during the early formative stages of a team or as new members are introduced throughout the project. The goal of the project leadership team is to quickly transition the individuals from a *group* to a *team*. During the forming stage of team development, members are typically inclined to be a bit formal and reserved. They are beginning to assess their level of comfort as colleagues and teammates. There is likely to be some anxiety about the ability of the team to perform, and there might be hints of alliances being formed.

The mission, objective, and rationale for the project are the object of high enthusiasm, but seem elusive and ambiguous. The forming stage is often characterized as an organizational honeymoon of sorts because team members have high morale and positive expectations. These positive feelings might be accompanied by anxiety and concern about why they are on the team, and about their specific roles and responsibilities. At this early stage, individuals are typically focused inward. Although they have feelings of excitement, anticipation, and optimism, and might be pleased they were selected for the project, there is still anxiety because the job ahead is mostly undefined.

During this stage, the project manager's job (with the support of the business analyst and other project leads) is to encourage people to not think of themselves as individuals but as team members by resolving issues about inclusion and trust. Team members may wonder why they were selected, what they have to offer, and how they will be accepted by colleagues new to them. Individuals have their own agendas at this stage because a team agenda has not yet been defined. It is during this stage that the team leaders present—and give the team members the opportunity to refine—the team vision, mission, and measures of success. Allowing the team members time and opportunity to express their feelings and collaborating to build team plans will help members begin to make the transition from a group of individuals to an effective team. During this stage, team members form opinions about whom they can trust and how much or how little involvement they will commit to the project.

Storming Stage

The storming stage emerges because team members likely have different opinions about how the team should operate. This stage can be disconcerting and is often thought to be nonproductive. However, going through the storming stage is helpful (and probably necessary) before moving on to more mature stages.

The storming stage is characterized by intra-group conflict. This is when boundaries and levels of authority are cemented within the group. In the best teams, natural leadership surfaces and conflict diminishes; in others, storming behaviors linger and need to be managed. Despite the name, this stage does not necessarily have to be highly emotional. There are times when it will be characterized by a higher-than-usual level of chaos as parties try to straighten out and evaluate their roles, their responsibilities, and the lines of communication.

Storming is generally seen as the most difficult stage in team development. It is the time when the team members begin to realize that the task is different or more difficult than they had imagined. Individuals experience some discrepancy between their initial hopes for the project and the reality of the situation. A sense of annoyance or even panic can set in. There are fluctuations in attitude about the team, one's role on the team, and the team's chances for success.

The goal of the team leaders is to quickly determine a subset of leaders and followers and to clarify roles and responsibilities so that the team will begin to congeal. Individuals will exert their influence, choose to follow others, or decide not to participate actively on the team. For those that choose to participate actively and exert their influence, interpersonal conflict might arise. Conflicts also might result between the team leaders and team members, particularly if the leadership is felt to be threatening or seen to be vulnerable or ineffective.

For team leaders who do not like dealing with conflict, the storming stage is the most difficult period to navigate. Although the inevitable conflict is sometimes destructive if not managed well, it can be positive. A conflict of ideas, raised in an environment of trust and openness, leads to higher levels of creativity and innovation.

The job of team leaders is to build a positive working environment, collaboratively set and enforce team ground rules that lead to open communication, and gently steer the team through this stage. The tendency is to rush through this stage as quickly as possible, often by pretending that a conflict does not exist. It is important to manage conflicts so they are not destructive. It is also important, however, to allow some conflict, because it is a necessary element of team maturation.

Norming Stage

Norming is typically the stage when work is underway. The team members, individually and collectively, have come together and established a group identity that allows them to work effectively together. Roles and responsibilities are clear, project objectives are understood, and progress is being made.

During this stage, communication channels likely have a good level of clarity and team members are adhering to agreed-upon rules of engagement during exchanges. Cooperation and collaboration replace the conflict and mistrust that characterized the previous stage.

As the project drags on, fatigue often sets in. Team leaders should look at both team composition and team processes to maintain continued motivation among members. Plan for short-term successes to create enthusiasm and sustained momentum. Celebrate and reward success at key milestones rather than waiting until the end of a long project. Continually capture lessons learned about how well the team is working together and implement suggested improvements.

Performing Stage

During the performing stage, team members tend to feel positive and excited about participating on the project. There is a feeling of urgency and a sense of confidence about the team's results. Conflicts are resolved using accepted practices. The team knows what it wants to do and revels in a sense of accomplishment as progress is made. Relationships and expectations are well-defined. There is genuine agreement among team members on their responsibilities. Team members have learned their roles and have discovered and accepted each others' strengths and weaknesses. Morale is at its peak during this stage, and the team has an opportunity to be high-performing.

During this stage, the best course of action for the team leaders is to lightly facilitate the work, consult and coach when necessary, encourage creativity, reward performance and achievement of goals, and generally stay out of the way. The performing stage of team development is what every team strives to achieve. It is difficult, however, to sustain this high level of performance for any length of time.

As we compare our project teams to high-performing teams outside the business environment (e.g., professional sports teams, heart transplant teams, special operations teams, paramedic teams, firefighters), what do high-performing teams have in common? They are small but mighty, highly trained and practiced, heavily invested in honing their skills, and they have a coach (sponsor) who removes barriers to success.

Some teams will reach and sustain high performance, optimizing their dynamic to become truly high-performing. Other teams might be in this stage sporadically or only within subsets of the team. It is a pleasure to observe and to be a part of high-performing teams when they occur.

Adjourning Stage

Adjourning can be thought of in the context of loss and closure. This stage of team development can be easily overlooked, as it occurs before and during a project or phase and for a short time after a project or phase is finished. During this stage of team development, the team conducts the tasks associated with disbanding the team and, to a certain extent, severs the everyday rhythm of their contacts and transactions.

There is some discomfort associated with this stage. Surprisingly, even teams that have had performance issues can experience sadness or grief during this closing stage. The project leadership team should act quickly to recognize the accomplishments of individuals and the team as a whole and to help team members transition to their next assignment.

Traversing the Team Development Stages

The stages of team development are very much an iterative dynamic. Any change in its make-up throws the team back to the very earliest stage of development, even if for a very short time. This is due to the natural evolution of teams, the addition of new members, removal of support, or changes in roles. The balancing and leveling of power is a constant dynamic in teams. As a member of the project leadership team, acquaint yourself with the cycles of team development, understand what the team is experiencing, and manage the implications of team development changes so that they have the most productive impact possible. Table 4-1 briefly characterizes the first four team development stages.

The shifting of practical power among the core leadership team members might cause the team to revert to the forming stage. Although this reversion might last only a short while, it is still a necessary part of the dynamics that help the team operate well. Team members then have to accustom themselves to the new order. The time spent in any of the stages subsequent to the reentry into forming can vary; but make no mistake, the team will experience storming again before regaining a foothold in the norming or performing stage.

Table 4-1—Team Development Stage Characteristics

Team Characteristics	Forming	Storming	Norming	Performing
Team Leader Style	Directing, presenting objectives, scope, and process to be followed	Supportive, active listening, managing conflict, driving consensus	Collaborative, shared leadership	Coaching, removing barriers
Team Member Behaviors	Tentative, slow to participate	Vying for position, conflict	Trust and respect for team members, support for leaders	Positive, professional, highly effective
Team Process	Driven by the team leader	Not working well due to conflict	Operating smoothly	Well-functioning and adapted as necessary
Trust	Low level	Alliances forming	Trusting relationships forming	High levels of trust, loyalty to the team develops
Decision-Making	Leaders make decisions	Difficulty making decisions, members unwilling to compromise	Consensus decision-making	Decisions made quickly by consensus, some decisions are delegated to subgroups or individuals

Team Leadership Roles through Stages

Many team development models are available to guide team development at any given point in the project life cycle. David C. Kolb, Ph.D., offers a five-stage team development model that provides team leadership strategies to use when developing the teams from their initial formation through to their actual performance.[8]

At each stage of the model, Kolb suggests that the business analyst and project manager continually adjust their leadership styles to maximize team effectiveness. He contends that a team leader subtly alters his or her style of team facilitation depending on the group's composition and level of maturity. The seasoned business analyst moves seamlessly between these team leadership modes as he or she observes and diagnoses the team's performance.

As mentioned in *The Art and Power of Facilitation: Running Powerful Meetings*, the business analyst needs to strive to acquire the leadership prowess described by Kolb and outlined in Table 4-2. It is even more important for the business analyst to know when and how to assume a particular team leadership role as teams move in and out of development phases during the life of the project.

Table 4-2—Five-Stage Team Development Model

Team Development Stage	Team Leadership Role
Building stage	Facilitator
Learning stage	Mediator
Trusting stage	Coach
Working stage	Consultant
Flowing stage	Collaborator

Facilitator

When the business analyst performs as the facilitator, the main goal is to provide the foundation for the team to make quality decisions. When the team first comes together, the business analyst uses expert facilitation skills to guide, direct, and develop the group. Requirements include understanding group dynamics, running effective meetings, facilitating dialog, and dealing with difficult behaviors. Facilitation skills include:

+ Understanding individual differences, work styles, and cultural nuances

+ Leading discussions and driving the group to consensus

+ Building a sense of team

+ Using and teaching collaborative skills

+ Managing meetings

+ Facilitating requirements workshops and focus groups

Mediator

Transitioning from facilitator to mediator poses a challenge for the new business analyst. It requires refrain from trying to control the team and lead the effort. The business analyst must be prepared to recognize when conflict is emerging (as it always does in teams) and be able to separate from it to mediate the situation. Although the facilitator does not have to resolve the conflict, he or she must help the team members manage it. Meditation skills (which are discussed at length in *The Art and Power of Facilitation: Running Powerful Meetings*) include:

+ Conflict management and resolution

+ Problem-solving and decision-making techniques

+ Idea-generation techniques

Coach

Coaching and mentoring take place at both the individual and team levels. Coaching is appropriate when trust has been established among the team members and communication is open and positive. The business analyst as coach uses experiences, perceptions, and intuition to help change team member behaviors and thinking. Coaching tasks include:

+ Setting goals

+ Teaching others how to give and receive feedback

+ Creating a team identity

+ Developing team decision-making skills

Consultant

As the team begins to work well together, the business analyst transitions into the role of consultant, providing advice, tools, and interventions to help the team reach its potential. The business analyst then concentrates on nurturing the team environment and solving problems. Consulting tasks include:

+ Assessing team opportunities

+ Supporting and guiding the team to create a positive, effective team environment

+ Aligning individual, team, and organizational values and strategic imperatives

+ Fostering team spirit

Collaborator

Few teams achieve an optimized level of teamwork and sustain it for long periods, because it is so intense. At this point, both the work and the leadership are shared equally among team members. The business analyst might hand off the lead role to team members as their expertise becomes the critical need during differing project activities. Collaboration skills include:

+ Leading softly

+ Sharing the leadership role

+ Assuming a peer relationship with team members

Clearly, project team leaders need to understand the dynamics of team development and adjust their leadership styles accordingly. Once a high-performing team has emerged, it is often necessary for the team leader to simply get out of the way.

Best Team-Building Practices for the Business Analyst

The business analyst has dual team-building requirements: (1) in general, he or she helps the other team leaders (the project manager, lead technologist, business visionary) build a high-performing project team; and (2) he or she is more directly responsible for building a high-performing *requirements* team.

As a member of the core project leadership team, the business analyst strives to help the core team members determine who should take the lead during different activities. For example, the project manager takes the lead during planning and status-update sessions. The business analyst leads requirements elicitation, analysis, review, and validation sessions. The business representative should assume the lead when talking about the business vision, strategy, and benefits expected from the new solution. The lead architect and/or developer leads discussions on technology trade-offs. The challenge is for the core leadership team to seamlessly traverse through the leadership handoffs so as not to interfere with the balance of the team.

More specifically, the business analyst leadership role involves forming and developing a high-performing requirements team by determining the appropriate business and technical representatives needed to traverse the requirements activities and securing approval to involve them.

As the requirements team comes together in workshop or review sessions, they are subjected to the same team development stages as the larger project team. The business analyst must deal with the challenges of each stage of team development. The goal for the business analyst is to optimize the dynamics and expertise of the requirements team members to foster innovation and creativity when determining the business requirements. Best practices include:

- Fostering the core team concept (small-but-mighty teams, co-located, working collaboratively)

- Building a solid, trusting relationship among the project team members and stakeholders

- Bringing in subject matter experts, subteams, and committees when needed to augment the core team

- Encouraging frequent (if possible, daily) meetings among the core team members

- Meeting face-to-face with customers often

- Devoting time to allow the requirements team to traverse the stages of team development

When forming the requirements team, spend enough time training it on the requirements practices and tools that will be used, so that the team members are comfortable with the process before they jump in head first.

As a project leader, the business analyst needs to focus on team dynamics and on building a high-performing team. It is not enough to develop requirements engineering knowledge and skills. It is also important to understand—and use—the power of teams.

Quick Team Assessment

In *Harnessing the Power of Teams*, Jim Clemmer states that "Despite all the team talk of the last few years, few groups are real teams. Too often they're unfocused and uncoordinated in their efforts."[9] Clemmer developed the following set of questions from his consulting and team development work. This team assessment and planning framework can be used to help newly formed teams come together and get productive quickly or to assist existing teams to refocus and renew themselves.

- Why do we exist (our purpose)?

- Where are we going (our vision)?

- How will we work together (our values)?

- Whom do we serve (internal or external customers or partners)?

- What is expected of us?

- What are our performance gaps (difference between the expectations and our performance)?

- What are our goals and priorities?

- What is our improvement plan?

- What skills do we need to develop?

- What support is available?

- How will we track our performance?

- How/when will we review, assess, celebrate, and refocus?

Use this approach to team building by having your team develop answers and action plans around each question.

Endnotes

1. Thomas A. Stewart. "The Corporate Jungle Spawns a New Species: The Project Manager." *Fortune*, July 1995: 179-180.

2. Jon R. Katzenbach and Douglas K. Smith. *The Wisdom of Teams: Creating the High-Performance Organization*, 1993. Boston: Harvard Business School Press.

3. Poppendieck, LLC. *Reflections on Development*, 2007. Online at http://www.poppendieck.com/development1.htm (accessed August 13, 2007).

4. Ibid.

5. Jon R. Katzenbach and Douglas K. Smith. *The Wisdom of Teams: Creating the High-Performance Organization*, 1993. Boston: Harvard Business School Press.

6. Ibid.

7. Bruce W. Tuckman. *Developmental Sequence in Small Groups, Psychological Bulletin* 63, no. 6 (June 1965): 384–399.

8. David C. Kolb. *Team Leadership*, 1999. Durango, CO: Lore International Institute.

9. Jim Clemmer. *Harnessing the Power of Teams*, 1999. Online at http://www.clemmer.net/articles/article_265.aspx (accessed August 17, 2007).

Chapter 5

The Business Analyst's Role in Communications

In This Chapter:

- Communication Building Blocks

- The Sender

- The Receiver

- Active Listening

- Miscommunication

- Best Communication Practices for the Business Analyst

Accurate, usable information is the currency of business analysis because the responsibility for planning and conducting requirements elicitation and validation sessions lies with the business analyst. The goal is to learn to use effective communication techniques that lead to clear, accurate information about the business requirements. While the responsibility for good communication is shared by all participants in the requirements sessions, the business analyst leads the way. The business analyst constantly looks for concerns and areas where confusion rather than clarity reigns.

To understand the critical skill sets that any business leader must have to communicate effectively, the communication process can be broken down to its basic elements. In this chapter, contributing author Kimi Ziemski discusses how important it is for the business analyst to understand and effectively use communication building blocks.

Communication Building Blocks

Communication is a process composed of building blocks used to get information from point A to point B. The basic components for both written and verbal communication are the same:

+ *Sender*—the person speaking or writing.

+ *Receiver*—the intended target for the message from the sender.

+ *Intent*—the internal concept or message the sender is trying to transmit to the receiver.

+ *Message*—what the receiver actually gets through sensory input, encrypted within the words used.

+ *Medium*—the way the message is verbally communicated—in writing, verbally, or physically (e.g., sign language, a welcoming wave hello).

+ *Encryption/Decryption*—the sender's translation of the intended message to accommodate the medium used to send the message. The receiver then translates it back. Encryption/decryption is simply the ability to understand the language used for the message.

Within each element of the communication process lurks the risk of miscommunication. Conflict resolution experts understand that it is not always a disagreement that causes conflict, but often a misunderstanding or miscommunication. The following sections discuss the communication elements in the context of the requirements elicitation process, focusing on the business analyst's communication skills.

The Sender

It's reasonable to assume that senders, business customers, and users who are the source of business requirements typically don't intend to create misunderstanding. Most of the time the sender has been working to make the message as clear as possible, and this fact usually contributes to the subsequent level of annoyance when the message is clearly not understood or received well by the business analyst.

The Intent

A sender's intended message—the intent—can be misunderstood, which may result in miscommunication. When the intent is to *educate*, the first challenge for the business analyst is that there are likely to be multiple levels of knowledge and expertise in the room in requirement elicitation sessions. Some people would suggest that the business analyst strives to bring the lowest levels in the room up to some sort of median before beginning to address the room at large. One strategy that can be used is to separate out the most knowledgeable people and use them as subject matter experts. Another approach is to establish separate times to talk with the different audiences.

If the intent is to *elicit information* (which is the cornerstone of business analysis), think about why the participants care about contributing information to the discussion. *What is in it for them?* The requirements elicitation process must take into account the possibility that participants may have very different agendas, perspectives, and priorities. The business analyst's role as a liaison between the various groups in an organization is to create an environment of collaboration and cooperation that facilitates the communication process. To maximize communication, learn to adopt a communication style that reflects the intended message most accurately.

The Message

How the business analyst frames messages impacts the response. During requirements elicitation workshops and focus groups, the business analyst documents the findings and sends them to all participants to review and provide feedback. When sending the draft outcome of the session for review, the messages you send can have either an *expanding effect* or a *narrowing effect* on the requirements under review.

If the team has not reached concrete conclusions about the business problem, or the participants have not yet provided the full input needed to be able to adequately articulate the requirement, craft your written message to stimulate expansion of thought processes, encourage exploration of possible interpretations, and promote a widening of perspectives.

If it is time to narrow the scope to a particular feature, convey the message that the team has completed the preliminary exploration and is now looking at a limited field of information to validate that the requirement under review is accurate, unambiguous, testable, and complete.

The Medium

The intent of communication is often signaled by the choice of the medium used to transmit the message. For the message to be received as intended, the sender must consider the intent, the message, *and* the medium, as well as the timing, image, and impact of the different mediums available.

Time constraints often dictate these choices. The constrained timeframes of today's business world have trained senders to use electronic mediums because they are so efficient and easy to use. The problem with the proliferation of email, instant messaging, and small messaging systems is that these methods are informal and highly impersonal. When it is time to validate captured requirements as accurate and complete, a face-to-face meeting is far superior to an email.

Encryption/Decryption

Encryption—selecting the language, tone, level of formality, and vocabulary that will best carry your message—is also an important consideration. The receiver decrypts messages when he or she demonstrates the ability to understand the true message and intent of the sender by rephrasing the message. A number of elements can prevent the receiver from being able to decrypt a message accurately. Because most of the effective communication in a message is based on elements that are not tied directly to the choice of vocabulary, such as tone and non-verbal body language, there is ample opportunity for faulty encryption or decryption.

Tailoring Communication to Individual Preferences and Styles

A key consideration in communicating effectively is the differences in personal and behavioral styles and preferences among the project stakeholders. Some people are get-to-the-point types, while others prefer to understand each nuance of context for the message. Some require little input to begin working their way to a conclusion, while others require more lengthy conversation and a more deliberate case built before coming to judgment or decision.

It is incumbent upon the business analyst to understand and account for these differing cultural and individual style preferences. The impact of cultural diversity on the business analyst's ability to be an effective liaison between business and technical professionals cannot be overstated. Culture in this context is not limited to ethnic, geographic, or national identity. Culture is also a function of our personal professional choices and of organizations as a whole.

Individual cultural preferences are influenced by the geographic areas we choose to live in as adults, and by how we reflect and interpret the experiences of our youth and childhood. Our cultural inclinations are demonstrated in how we relate to people, issues, and group pressures. Cultural predispositions are revealed when we react to situations and in how we choose to initiate action. The culmination of all cultural influences on our lives can also be seen in how we communicate—and when we don't. Cultural influences dictate how much context a user or customer representative requires to be comfortable enough to be willing to listen and participate in requirements elicitation sessions. The business analyst considers these cultural differences when planning and facilitating group requirements sessions.

The Receiver

The ability to listen well is of particular importance to the business analyst when discussing business concepts with the technical team members, and when presenting technical concepts to a business audience. It is the business analyst who interprets requirements stated by stakeholders and confirms that the requirements are understood in the same way by both the business and technical teams.

Chief among the receiver's responsibilities is to respond to the sender by interpreting the message and revealing how clearly the message came across. Validation and confirmation of the message are essential to effective communication. When facilitating sessions, the business analyst listens closely to the message and to the choice of verbiage and tone and then rephrases the message to demonstrate that it has been heard. After transcribing the content of the message on a flip chart or white board, the business analyst once again checks with the sender to confirm that it has been accurately captured and then asks the full group if it needs additional clarification or discussion, or if it concurs.

Active Listening

There are often competing demands on the time and mental energy of project stakeholders. Active listening suggests that the business analyst focus on the message that the user/customer intended, and assume the role of receiver in an interactive way. Active listening consists of *intent, action,* and *confirmation.*

Intent

During requirements elicitation and validation sessions, the business analyst often acts as the receiver. In that role, the business analyst focuses closely on the intentions of the person sending the message. The goal is to focus on listening and attempting to *really hear* what that person is saying.

Action

When it is clear that the sender has completed the message, the business analyst takes action to clarify, question, and confirm to ensure that the thought has been fully heard and understood. Hints of concerns or issues that are contained in the initial transmission are discussed fully until both parties agree to a description or statement of the requirement.

Confirmation

Confirmation is the action taken when the business analyst summarizes or paraphrases the message to confirm that the message has been received and is understood. Once the sender agrees with the confirmation, the business analyst can move on.

The time required for full confirmation—especially during requirements elicitation—is often called into question when first practiced because it seems to take longer than the standard exchange of information. Keep in mind, however, that the use of active listening reduces the amount of time spent managing changes to requirements later in the process.

As with any new skill set, active listening is something that some people can do better than others. The business analyst can improve his or her competency level with practice and focus. When the participants in requirements sessions have been truly listened to, they feel acknowledged and validated. It is a sign of respect to give concrete acknowledgment of having heard someone's position.

Miscommunication

Several factors can contribute to miscommunication. The effective business analyst understands these factors, and makes appropriate accommodations.

+ *Ineffective verbal or written communication skills.* It is entirely possible that the sender (the person attempting to articulate the requirement) lacks the necessary competency level to communicate complex or technical issues to the group. *Suggestion:* Practice talking with people new to the field or industry to get a fresh perspective on their conversational and business verbal styles. Apply lessons learned when facilitating requirements elicitation and review meetings.

+ *Assumptions of requisite knowledge.* The assumption that because something is painfully obvious to us, it is just as clearly obvious to others can cause a deep valley of misunderstanding. *Suggestion:* As you work with subject matter experts, ask yourself what information you would assume they already know. Examine the possibility that you might not get another opportunity to talk with the experts before finalizing requirements, so be certain to clarify your understanding.

+ *Reluctance to infer that the recipient is not knowledgeable.* It is always valid to care about the way your message is being received. It is this very concern that can help you craft your message to make sure it is effectively received. *Suggestion*: Establish an environment where people can feel comfortable asking questions, clarifying areas of concern, and airing differences of opinion. Facilitate the flow of information as it unfolds by transcribing it on poster paper or a white board. Check periodically to make sure that all parties are operating with the same understanding of the information. Most of all, remember that in your role as a business analyst, it is your responsibility to translate business needs into business requirements and ensure that the communication channels are clear.

+ *Too many communication channels.* Communication channels must be maintained for every stakeholder group. The communication complexity increases as more stakeholders are added. *Suggestion*: When crafting your message, try to articulate the main points in multiple ways. Each recipient has a personal frame of reference, and sometimes hearing the same information presented in multiple ways helps the whole group find a common understanding. It is for this reason that business analysts strive to document requirements in multiple ways, including with text, diagrams, models, lists, matrices, and tables.

Best Communication Practices for the Business Analyst

If the communication that takes place during the requirements elicitation process is improved, the results can potentially provide payback in terms of reduced rework and a higher quality solution that truly meets the needs of the business. Most requirements techniques focus on specification (representation of the requirements). To ensure that quality communication has transpired during requirements elicitation, incorporate these best practices:

+ Collaborate with the project manager and other core team members to build the requirements elicitation and communication plan; include communication to key requirement stakeholders.

+ Continually evaluate the effectiveness of the requirements elicitation and communication strategies.

+ Continually validate the requirements with the customer and other stakeholder groups through evaluation, integration, prioritization, reviews, walk-throughs, and reviews of requirements understanding models.

+ Execute a simple, straightforward communication plan using forceful and convincing messages sent through many channels.

+ Visualize and communicate requirements in the right way to the right audience. Create a blueprint (a view or conceptual model; a rich picture) of what the solution will cover. It is the starting point for defining the phasing of critical and non-critical functionality.

+ Build prototypes and "a day in the life" scenarios.

+ Use technology to share information, e.g., video recordings of current user operations; webcasts of business vision and rationale for change; and live, interactive usability testing.

Accurate and complete requirements depend on the business analyst's ability to foster understanding among different perspectives, areas of expertise, and communication styles. This is a tall order, since effective communication demands acquisition of particular knowledge, skills, and experience. Senior business analysts are consummate communicators. Of all of the skills needed to be an effective business analyst, communication is perhaps the most critical. It is of utmost importance that business analysts understand and use effective communication techniques.

Chapter 6

Customer Relationship Management: Politics and Stakeholders

In This Chapter:

- Power and Politics
- Stakeholder Identification
- Stakeholder Categorization
- Best Stakeholder Management Practices for the Business Analyst

In this chapter, contributing author Richard Vander Horst discusses how important it is for the business analyst to understand project stakeholders, analyze their ability to influence the success of the project, and operate effectively in the context of the power and politics that are always present in the organization.

Power and Politics

One of the most important responsibilities for a business analyst is to identify key stakeholders—individuals and groups who are involved in or will be impacted by the project—and draw them appropriately into the requirements definition and validation activities. Three primary truths are key to this responsibility:

- *Politics are real.* Whenever groups of people are involved, there are politics manifested in views and opinions that drive behaviors. To suppose that a project will not be affected by politics is unrealistic and will ultimately degrade your ability to deliver quality results.

Humans are fairly predictable and, when left to the influences of evolution and culture, will succumb to the pressures and allure of power and control. That is not to say that best intentions are not always at play, for they usually are; the question comes down to whether the best intentions of participants are aligned with the project goals and objectives.

The challenge for the business analyst and other project leaders is to acknowledge that the project will be affected by politics and power struggles, and to implement strategies to manage the political dynamics by: (1) conducting an analysis to determine those who can influence the project, and whether they feel positively or negatively about the project; (2) identifying the goals of the key influencers; and (3) defining problems, solutions, and action plans to take advantage of positive political influences and to neutralize negative ones.

- *Know and involve project stakeholders.* Involving stakeholders within the organization undergoing change and planning to make sure that power and politics do not adversely affect the project objectives is critical to successful execution of projects. All too often, when project teams see themselves as agents of change, they ignore the fact that they are attempting to bring about change to an existing and culturally entrenched environment.

Culture is defined as the attitudes and behaviors that are characteristic of a particular organization. The culture and philosophy of the organization undergoing change will not flex to meet the needs of the project; the project will need to be adapted to the existing culture of the organization.

Successful change initiatives are dependent on many factors: (1) the change must align with the goals of the organization, (2) key influencers within the organization must be involved in designing and implementing the change, and (3) unique perspectives and organizational readiness for the change must be taken into account.

+ *Solution value and sustainability are key measures of success.* Deploying the new business solution within time and cost constraints is traditionally considered *the* major accomplishment to achieve project success. However, the value added to the organization as a result of the new business solution is the true measure of project success. If the solution is delivered on time, within budget, and with the full scope of features, but does not add the expected value to the organization, then the project has actually failed.

To ensure that the project outcomes add the expected value, a project team must understand the long-term goals of the organization and how the deliverables of the project will help advance those goals. A sustainable solution emerges when the project team respects the political landscape, understands the culture of the organization, and ensures that the solution is strategically aligned with the goals of the organization. Many successfully executed projects are celebrated upon completion, only to reveal later that very little of the solution was actually applicable and effective as intended.

When these three truths guide project team decisions, they form the basis for how to deal with the politics and stakeholders surrounding the project. Politics are real, and they exist in every project with virtually no exceptions. Failure to recognize the impact of power and politics will likely result in a failed project.

Finally, remember that completing a project within time, cost and scope constraints is not success; success is delivering a new business solution that meets the business need, advances organizational strategies, adds measurable value, and is sustainable over time.

Stakeholder Identification

The first step in any stakeholder management process is to identify all stakeholders. The *PMBOK® Guide* defines a stakeholder as "any person or group that is actively involved in the project, whose interests may be positively or negatively affected by the execution or completion of the project, or may exert influence over the project and its deliverables."[1] Stakeholder identification is a collaborative effort among the core project leadership team (business analyst, project manager, and business and technical leads).

Stakeholders come in all shapes and sizes, from the executive sponsor of the project to the end user of the solution. Functional managers provide resources to the project, executives fund the project, project managers, business analysts, and business and technical representatives are responsible for the success of the project, and project team members design and develop the solution. Stakeholders also include clients, customers, and end users of the new solution delivered by the project, as well as IT staff members who operate and maintain the technical components of the solution.

All key stakeholders will likely want to see the project be successful. However, stakeholders undoubtedly have differing perspectives, and therefore differing definitions of success. The project leadership should encourage all perspectives toward clear, measurable success criteria.

When attempting to identify project stakeholders, look for individuals or groups that are likely asking questions about their involvement in the project. Stakeholder interests typically fall into three categories: (1) interest in their contributions to the project, (2) interest in the benefits they receive as a result of the project, and (3) interest in any other effects the project is likely to have on them.

Stakeholders interested about their contributions to the project usually supply money, people, time, energy, or some other sort of resource. Stakeholders interested in what they may receive as a result of the project are likely the recipients of the new solution, including executives who want to achieve the expected business benefits provided by the solution. These two groups of stakeholders tend to be the easiest to identify, analyze, and manage.

The third category of stakeholders—those interested in any other effects the project will have on them—tends to be less obvious or visible. For example, there may be multiple groups of end users who have differing—and sometimes conflicting—requirements for the solution. Or there may be stakeholders that are ancillary to the organization undergoing change or stakeholders that are represented by someone else. Other stakeholders are not directly impacted by the project, but are competing for the same resources. Others may be involved in a subsequent project that depends on outcomes of the current project.

As the project leadership team begins to identify project stakeholders, it is helpful to first identify reliable sources of information. One source of information is the organization's master project schedule. The master schedule should reveal what other projects are currently underway or planned for the future. The strategic plans, goals, objectives, and success measures should help determine how closely a project matches corporate goals; close alignment will hopefully encourage strong executive stakeholder support.

It is also helpful to review all corporate organization charts depicting the relationships between the different units of the company.

These documents could clarify the direct and indirect business units related to a project. Finally, always fall back on basic elicitation skills, identifying obvious stakeholders and project team members early, and continue to locate other, less-obvious stakeholders throughout the requirements engineering process.

Stakeholder Categorization

After identifying stakeholders, categorize them as groups or individuals according to how they may be positively or negatively affected by the execution or completion of the project. Categorizing stakeholders also helps determine the appropriate level and type of involvement for each individual or group, and assists in developing strategies for stakeholder management. It is helpful to categorize stakeholders according to their interests. In general there are three types of stakeholders:

+ *Project-Oriented Stakeholders*—project team members who have no long-term benefits or involvement in the use of the new business solution. They must, however, have a full understanding of the business value the project is intended to add to the organization.

+ *Business-Oriented Stakeholders*—less involved in the project itself; the beneficiaries of the outcome of the project or the solution it delivers.

+ *Project- and Business-Oriented Stakeholders*—have an interest in both the successful execution of the project, and are beneficiaries of the outcome of the project or the solution it delivers.

Categorization in this manner allows the business analyst to identify project stakeholders that are likely to be highly invested in the accurate and complete definition of requirements. In his or her leadership role, the business analyst is responsible for ensuring that the outcome of the project will meet or exceed the needs of the ultimate customer and deliver the projected business value—and this cannot be accomplished without collaboration with key stakeholders.

Project-Oriented Stakeholders

Project-oriented stakeholders are focused solely on the completion of the project on time and within budget. This group includes the functional managers of the performing organization who allocate resources to the project and project team members themselves. While a project must balance the competing demands of time, cost, scope, risk, and quality, success is dependent on getting requirements right. A project-oriented stakeholder is more likely to want to reduce the scope and/or adjust the quality of the solution in order to keep the cost and schedule on track. This can be in conflict with the goals of the business analyst.

If functional managers perceive the project as productive because it is staying on time, keeping within budget, and making good use of resources, they will tend to support the project. If, however, the project begins to experience challenges, they may begin to withdraw support. Manage this group through frequent status updates with factual information. When it's necessary to present bad news about project progress to this group, be sure to recommend a corrective action plan as well.

Business-Oriented Stakeholders

Business-oriented stakeholders own and operate the new business solution, including the members of business units impacted by the change and executives who approved and funded the initiative. These stakeholders are more aligned with the business analyst because they ultimately will have to use or leverage the new solution to provide value through the organization to the customers and shareholders to improve business performance.

Business-oriented stakeholders can be an invaluable resource to the business analyst because the business analyst continually re-examines the business case to ensure continued investment in the project is warranted during project execution. Also, the business analyst is measuring actual business benefits achieved versus costs to build and/or acquire and operate the system after deployment.

The stakeholders benefiting from the new business solution are typically interested in seeing a positive outcome from a quality standpoint. They will tend to be a close ally of the business analyst when eliciting and specifying requirements, and should be involved in key decisions affecting the quality of the new solution or the business case. This group may exert a positive influence over the other groups of stakeholders, helping to resolve disagreements about business requirements through negotiation and compromise.

Project- and Business-Oriented Stakeholders

The business analyst is likely to find strong allies in business- and project-oriented stakeholders as well. While they are involved in the project in some capacity, they also have a vested interest in the operability and sustainability of the new business solution.

This group includes the business and technical representatives assigned to the project who will operate and maintain the business and technical components of the solution after it is deployed. These stakeholders help provide the insight required to balance the competing demands of the project.

Unidentified Stakeholders

Unidentified stakeholders can cause unwelcome and adverse impacts to the project. If stakeholder groups or individuals are not identified, there may be missing or incorrect requirements. In addition, groups impacted by but not involved appropriately in the project may attempt to exert a negative influence over the project.

If this happens, address the issue immediately, soliciting support from others who feel positive about the project. Managing disgruntled stakeholders requires the ability to enlist support from other stakeholders.

Best Stakeholder Management Practices for the Business Analyst

The ability to manage stakeholders can make or break a project. The following leadership practices will help business analysts partner with other key project leaders to identify and manage stakeholders effectively:

- Revisit the list of stakeholders often to continually validate that no individual or group has been overlooked.

- Continually validate the effectiveness of the stakeholder management strategies.

- Uphold personal integrity and honesty.

- After identifying key stakeholders and developing a political management strategy, work with stakeholder groups to reduce complacency, fear, and anger over the change, and to increase their sense of urgency.

- Build a guidance team of supporters who have the credibility, skills, connections, reputations, and formal authority to provide necessary leadership.

- Use the guidance team to develop a clear, simple, compelling vision and set of strategies to achieve the vision.

- Execute a simple, straight-forward communication plan using forceful and convincing messages sent through many channels. Use the guidance team to promote the vision whenever possible.

+ Use the guidance team to remove barriers to change, including disempowering management styles, antiquated business processes, and inadequate access to information.

+ Plan the delivery of the solution to achieve early successes. Wins create enthusiasm and momentum.

+ When the project is dependent on major deliverables from other projects currently underway within the organization, the core project team should identify and manage such deliverables. Assign someone from a core team as the *dependency owner*, to liaise with the team creating the deliverable. A best practice is for dependency owners to attend team meetings of the dependent project, so as to demonstrate the importance of the dependency and to hear status updates first hand.

While on the surface it may appear that project goals are shared by all, different stakeholders will likely have different and competing expectations. The business analyst should identify stakeholders who are focused on the long-term business benefits resulting from project outcomes. Doing so will greatly improve the business analyst's ability to create a support structure within the team that has the authority and influence to ensure that the needs of the business are well understood and documented.

Endnote

1. Project Management Institute. *Guide to the Project Management Body of Knowledge*, 3rd ed., 2004. Newtown Square, PA: Project Management Institute, Inc.

Part III

Getting There

*I*n this final section, we discuss two critical areas: the development of individual business analysts and the maturity of organizational business analysis capabilities.

In Chapter 7 we provide insights into how an individual business analyst can carve out a leadership role in an organization.

In Chapter 8 we present the case for establishing a business analysis center of excellence in your organization.

Chapter 7

Carving Out Your Leadership Role

In This Chapter:

- Leadership Development for the Business Analyst
- The Business-Savvy and Technically Savvy Business Analyst
- Business Analyst Leadership Opportunities
- Getting There

The global marketplace has significant impact on professionals working to build and sustain careers in the ever-changing modern work environment. To succeed in today's workforce, it's important to welcome change, develop strong leadership skills, and embrace life-long learning. Careers are very different than they were in the twentieth century. Successful careers in today's environment are more dynamic than in the past, when people tended to move up rather narrow functional hierarchies, performing essentially the same job function for most of their careers.

Many of today's professionals cling to the twentieth-century career model that says if you are a good employee, you will succeed and grow within one organization and within a single job category. Many of us don't think in terms of developing our leadership potential and helping our organizations cope with the transformation process from functional hierarchies to team-based work. Clearly, organizations are beginning to value business analysis leadership skills, realizing that they are essential not only to manage critical projects but also to deal with organizational change.

Leadership Development for the Business Analyst

Many strategies promote lifelong learning and exploration of personal leadership potential, including:

+ *Joining professional associations.* Participate in professional organizations, conferences, and workshops, especially those associated with the International Institute of Business Analysis (IIBA).[1]

+ *Training.* Acquire business analysis knowledge and skills through formal courses.

+ *Networking.* Build a strong network and continually seek feedback from peers and subordinates.

+ *Mentoring.* Seek out a trustworthy person to serve as a personal mentor. Likewise, provide coaching and mentoring to new business analysts.

+ *Gaining experience.* Voluntarily participate in initiatives and projects beyond your current assignments.

+ *Volunteering.* Become involved as a volunteer and leader in community and nonprofit organizations to test personal leadership capabilities. Trying to produce results through people without having a position of authority is one of the best opportunities to test personal leadership skills.

+ *Reading.* Do extensive professional reading, not only to deepen personal expertise in leadership, project management, business analysis, information technology, and in a certain business domain, but also to acquire familiarity with associated fields.

The Business-Savvy and Technically Savvy Business Analyst

Senior business analysts are an invaluable asset to organizations that are constantly undergoing change. Focus on the following topics to become a *business-savvy* leader:

+ Industry expertise

+ Business domain (e.g., finance, human resources, engineering, supply chain)

+ Organizational structures, culture, power, and politics

+ Strategic thinking

+ Process paths across functional areas

+ General management

+ Interpersonal skills; influencing skills

Senior business analysts function seamlessly as they traverse the boundaries from the business to the technical communities. Focus on the following topics to become a *technically savvy* leader:

+ The role of IT in achieving strategic vision

+ Business application knowledge, standards, and regulations

+ The project environment

+ The project management body of knowledge

+ The business analysis body of knowledge

Business analysts who are valued as strategic assets seize opportunities to make themselves visible and to influence executives. Opportunities abound for those who have business analysis expertise.

Business Analyst Leadership Opportunities

It is an exciting time for business analysts, since the profession of business analysis is just now emerging. Senior business analysts carve out their own leadership role. As they begin to acquire leadership skills, they create opportunities to influence executives, gaining experience while making themselves visible to senior members of the organization. Opportunities include participation in or leading the following activities:

- *Studies.* Conduct competitive and benchmarks studies, generate results, and write implications reports.

- *New business opportunities.* Identify and define new business opportunities.

- *Business case development.* Prepare decision packets for new project proposals.

- *Stage-gate reviews.* Prepare for and facilitate control gate reviews.

- *Stakeholder management.* Identify stakeholder management problems, symptoms, and strategies.

- *Customer relationship management.* Identify customer management problems, symptoms, and strategies.

Leadership opportunities also exist to develop and promote the business analysis profession. The business analysis center of excellence (BACoE) is becoming an important vehicle for advancing the maturity of business analysis practices within an organization (Chapter 8 discusses BACoEs at length.) In addition, local IIBA chapters are actively seeking volunteers to assume leadership positions. Volunteer positions are an effective way to acquire and test leadership skills and techniques.

Getting There

Staffing surveys reveal an increasing demand for senior project managers and business analysts. As these project leaders are assigned to complex projects, it is essential that they be prepared for the challenge.

Project Leader Knowledge and Skill Requirements

Considerable knowledge and skills are required to manage complex projects. Table 7-1 presents the array of competencies required to lead complex projects.[2]

Table 7-1—Skill Requirements for Senior Project Manager and Business Analyst

Technical	Analytical	Business	Leadership
Use of technology to support business objectives	Use of project life cycles to deliver valuable solutions quickly	Strategic planning, goal setting, measurement	Customer relationship management
Systems engineering concepts and principles	Business analysis	Business process improvement and reengineering	Project, program, and portfolio management
Powerful modeling techniques	Ability to conceptualize and think creatively	Business planning	Capacity to articulate vision
Communication of technical concepts to non-technical audiences	Techniques to plan, elicit, analyze, specify, validate, trace and manage requirements	Communication of business concepts to technical audiences	Organizational change management; management of power and politics
Testing, verification, and validation	Requirements risk assessment and management	Business outcome thinking	Problem solving, negotiation, and decision-making
Technical writing	Administrative, analytical, and reporting skills	Business writing	Team management, leadership, mentoring, facilitation, meeting management

Table 7-1—Skill Requirements for Senior Project Manager and Business Analyst (continued)

Technical	Analytical	Business	Leadership
Rapid prototyping	Cost/benefit analysis	Business case development	Authenticity, ethics, and integrity
Technical domain knowledge	Time and cost management and personal organization	Business domain knowledge	Project benefits management

Project Leader Career Path

As organizations depend more and more on successful project outcomes to achieve their strategic goals, they are developing career paths for their project managers and business analysts. Table 7-2 presents a generic project manager/business analyst career path.

Table 7-2—Project Manager and Business Analyst Career Path

Level	Proficiency	Responsibilities	Competencies
Strategic	Ability to perform strategic tasks with minimal direction	Lead large, highly complex projects	• Business & IT strategy • Program and portfolio mgt. • Systems engineering, BPR, Six Sigma • Enterprise architecture • Business case development
Senior	Ability to perform complex tasks with minimal coaching	Lead moderately complex projects	• Business & IT domains • Advanced project management & business analysis • Systems engineering, BPR, Six Sigma • Requirements engineering

Table 7-2—Project Manager and Business Analyst Career Path (continued)

Level	Proficiency	Responsibilities	Competencies
Intermediate	Ability to perform simple-to-moderately complex tasks with minimal assistance	Lead small, independent projects	• Business &/or IT domain • Fundamentals of project management & business analysis • Quality management • Facilitation & meeting management • Basic requirements modeling
Associate	Ability to perform simple tasks with assistance	Support intermediate and senior PM/BAs	• PM/BA principles • BPR, Six Sigma principles • Business writing

Project Leader Assignments Mapped to Project Complexity

To make appropriate project leadership assignments, project complexity must be considered. The Project Management and Business Analyst Organizational Maturity Model (discussed in greater detail in Chapter 8) in Figure 7-1 shows that in addition to large, highly complex projects, strategic-level business analysts manage requirements for programs (a group of projects managed in a coordinated way to obtain greater benefits) and portfolios (a collection of projects or programs managed together to achieve strategic goals).

Organizations depend on successful projects to seize or sustain competitive advantage, and ultimately achieve their strategies. Managing projects in highly competitive and changing circumstances requires technical experts and business visionaries to work with project leaders who possess a combination of skills including leadership, management, project management, and business analysis.

Figure 7-1—Project Manager and Business Analyst Organizational Maturity Model

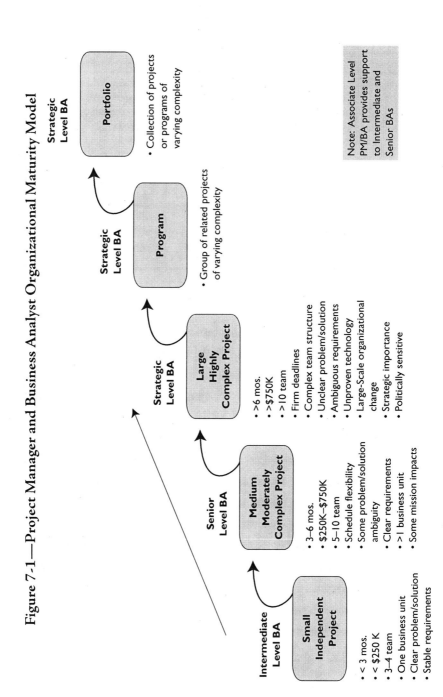

Endnotes

1. The IIBA is an international not-for-profit association for business analysis professionals. The IIBA's vision is to be the leading worldwide professional association that develops and maintains standards for the practice of business analysis and for the certification of practitioners. This fledgling organization is growing rapidly, and if you blink, you will miss out on building the foundations of the business analysis profession. The International Institute of Business Analysis (IIBA), online at www.theiiba.org.

2. This list was derived from a survey of job descriptions appearing on the website Monster.com®. Monster.com® is a company helping job seekers search available jobs and access career information and advice, and helping employers access hiring tools to streamline the hiring process. To search for the kind of project management and business analysis job information referenced in Table 7-1, go to http://www.monster.com/ and enter in job-related key words and phrases like "senior project manager" next to the job search caption.

Chapter 8

Establishing a Business Analysis Center of Excellence

In This Chapter:

- Centers of Excellence

- Business Analysis Centers of Excellence (BACoE)

- BACoE Scope Considerations

- BACoE Organizational Positioning Considerations

- BACoE Organizational Maturity Considerations

- BACoE Implementation Considerations

- BACoE Implementation Best Practices

- Final Words of Wisdom

Centers of Excellence

Centers of excellence are emerging as vital strategic assets to serve as the primary vehicle for managing complex change initiatives, and are being recognized as a business support function just as critical as accounting, marketing, finance, and human resources. A *center of excellence* (CoE) is a team of people that is established to promote collaboration and the application of best practices.[1]

CoEs exist to bring an enterprise focus to many business issues, including data integration, project management, enterprise architecture, business and IT optimization, and enterprise-wide access to information. The concept of CoEs is quickly maturing in twenty-first century organizations because of the need to collaboratively determine solutions to complex business issues. The project management office (PMO), a type of CoE, proliferated in the 1990s as a centralized approach to managing projects.

Industry leaders are effectively using various types of CoEs.

Hewlett-Packard Service-Oriented Architecture

Hewlett-Packard (HP) uses a service-oriented architecture (SOA) as a CoE when implementing large-scale organizational change for its clients. The SOA is a breakthrough software design technique that allows the development of smaller "services" (groups of software components that perform business processes). The services are then hooked together with other services to perform larger tasks. The services are loosely coupled, have an independent interface to the core system, and are reusable. Web services, for example, constitute an SOA, and are an important strategy to increase business and reduce transaction costs.

SOA represents a transformation in how businesses and IT develop business solutions. It is an effort to drive down the total cost of ownership of IT systems, thus freeing scarce resources to develop innovative IT applications and infrastructures. HP describes its CoEs as a critical component of large-scale organizational change. It looks upon its SOA CoEs as SWAT teams that are fully focused on implementing the reusable service-oriented components and infrastructure.[2]

SOA CoEs provide many of the same benefits offered by business analysis centers of excellence (BACoEs):

+ Establish enterprise standards, procedures, governance

+ Standardize infrastructure, development methods, and operational procedures

+ Increase business agility (i.e., the ability to adapt quickly as the environment changes)

+ Reduce risk, complexity, and redundancy

+ Align business and IT units

+ Enable reuse and faster time-to-market

+ Present one face to the customer

IBM Centers of Excellence

IBM is also heavily invested in CoEs. The IBM project management CoE is dedicated to defining and executing the steps needed to strengthen IBM's project management capabilities. The IBM project management CoE (PMCoE) strives to combine external industry trends with internal insight to develop project management policy, practices, methods, and tools.

The IBM PMCoE has experienced such success that in 2006 IBM announced the creation of new CoEs to help customers better use information. These CoEs will facilitate software and service experts in the development of six new solution portfolios: business analysis and discovery, master data management, business process innovation, risk and compliance, workforce productivity, business performance, and process management. These centers will develop products and services to better implement business analysis practices. Their goal is to help organizations transform information from utility for running the business to a competitive asset.[3]

Business Analysis Centers of Excellence

Centers of excellence are becoming invaluable to successful management of large-scale change. The business analysis center of excellence (BACoE) is emerging as an industry best practice, too. The BACoE is a new type of center that serves as the single point of contact for business analysis practices. In that role, the BACoE defines the business rules, processes, knowledge, skills, competencies, and tools used by organizations to perform business analysis activities throughout the business solution life cycle.

As the discipline of business analysis becomes professionalized, it is no surprise that BACoEs are now emerging. Staffed with knowledgeable business and IT teams, these centers are fulfilling a vital need in organizations today by providing a business-focused home for current business analysis practices, technologies, and emerging trends.

The BACoE serves as an internal consultant and information broker to both the project teams and the executive management team. In addition, the BACoE is responsible for continuous improvement of business analysis practices. Toward that end, the BACoE continually evaluates the maturity of business analysis and implements improvements to overall business analysis capability.

A 2006 white paper from SAP America, Inc., an enterprise software and services company that specializes in business intelligence, enterprise resource planning, customer relationship management, and supply chain management applications, describes the value of CoEs:

> Organizations with centralized CoEs have better consistency and coordination, leading directly to less duplication of effort. These organizations configure and develop their IT systems by business

process or functional area rather than by business unit, leading to more efficient and more streamlined systems operations.[4]

Best-in-class CoEs evaluate the impact of proposed changes on all areas of the business and effectively allocate resources and support services according to business priorities.

To achieve a balanced perspective, it is important to involve other groups in the design of the BACoE, including business operations, IT (e.g., enterprise architects, database managers, infrastructure support teams, service-level managers, capacity and availability managers, application developers), PMO representatives and project managers, and representatives from the project governance group.

If an organization already has one or more CoEs, consider combining them into one centralized center focused on program and project excellence. The goal is for a cross-functional team of experts (business visionary, technology expert, project manager, business analyst) to address the full solution life cycle from business case development to continuous improvement and support of the solution for all major projects.

A BACoE Success Story

One successful BACoE is at the Bank of Montreal (BMO). According to Kathleen Barret, senior business consultant at BMO Financial Group and president of the IIBA, the center's formation began in early 2002.[5] By October 2003 the center had conducted a current-state assessment, developed, piloted, and released its business analysis process standard, and received certification for their processes through the International Standards Organization (ISO). By 2005 its business analysis training and accreditation program had been rolled out.

Barret noted the following guidelines were critical to the successful implementation of the BMO center:

+ Identify specific goals and deadlines (e.g., ISO certification by a certain date).

+ Treat the CoE implementation effort like a project: create a formal project team with a steering committee.

+ Ensure senior executive support and enforcement of new practices.

+ Link outcomes to performance pay.

+ Adopt a formal approach to measure and evaluate compliance with standards.

+ Involve all stakeholder areas—include everyone and overlook no one.

+ Adopt best practices from within the organization.

+ Provide process training to all practitioners and team members.

+ Communicate at multiple levels, in words that mean something to each group.

There are many considerations that must be taken into account when establishing a new CoE, including its scope in terms of disciplines and functions, organizational alignment, placement and maturity, and the implementation approach.

BACoE Scope Considerations

BACoEs vary in their composition and scope. Some organizations are focused across the entire project life cycle, whereas others focus more narrowly on requirements engineering. A center of requirements excellence, for example, improves skills needed for requirements elicitation, analysis, specification, and validation.

A truly comprehensive BACoE, however, is broadly scoped to in-clude the services, functions, tools, and metrics necessary to ensure that the organization invests in the most valuable projects, and that those projects deliver the expected business benefits. Figure 8-1 pro-vides a summary of typical BACoE functions.

One of the critical BACoE functions is *benefits management*, a continuous process of identifying new opportunities, envisioning results, implementing, checking intermediate results, and dynami-cally adjusting the path leading from investments to business results. Business and technology experts typically staff BACoEs, acting as central points of contact and facilitating collaboration among busi-ness and IT groups.

The role of BACoEs is multidimensional and usually includes the following components: (1) it provides thought leadership for all initiatives to confirm that the organization's business analysis standards are maintained and adhered to; (2) it conducts feasibility studies and prepares business cases for proposed new projects; (3) it participates in the leadership of all strategic initiatives by provid-ing expert business analysis resources; and (4) it conducts benefits management to ensure that strategic change initiatives provide the value to the organization that was expected.

Strategic BACoE

A fully functioning BACoE is capable of providing services across the gamut of business analysis practices by training, consulting, and mentoring business analysts and project team members, providing business analysis resources to the project teams, facilitating the port-folio management process, and serving as the custodian of business analysis best practices.

Figure 8-1—BACoE Function Chart

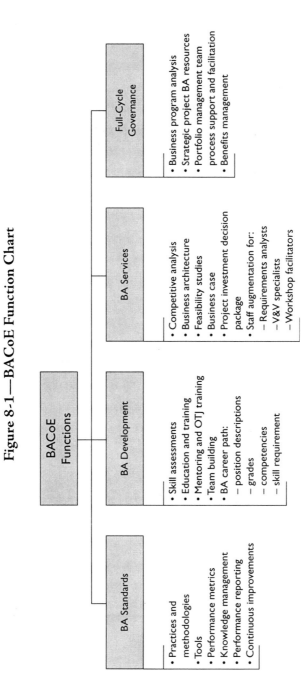

The strategic BACoE generally performs all or a subset of the following services:

+ *Business analysis standards.*

  □ *Methods.* Defines the methodology, metrics, and tools for use on all strategic projects within the organization.

  □ *Knowledge management.* Maintains the central historical database of business analysis standard tools, processes, and business architecture components.

  □ *Continuous improvement.* Periodically evaluates the maturity of the business analysis practices within the organization and implements improvements to policies, processes, tools, and procedures.

+ *Business analyst development.*

  □ *Business analyst career path.* Along with the human resources department, designs and maintains the project manager competency model, including titles, position descriptions, and functions.

  □ *Coaching and mentoring.* Provides mentoring services to business analysts and project teams to help them meet the challenges of their current project.

  □ *Training and professional development.* Provides formal skills and knowledge assessments, and education and training for the professional development of business analysts.

  □ *Team building.* Provides team-building experiences to project managers, business analysts, and team members.

+ *Business analysis services.* Serves as a group of facilitators and on-the-job trainers that are skilled and accomplished business analysts to provide business analysis consulting support, including:

- *Studies.* Conducting market research, benchmark and feasibility studies

- *Business architecture.* Developing and maintaining the business architecture

- *Business case.* Preparing and monitoring the business case

- *Requirements engineering.* Eliciting, analyzing, specifying, documenting, validating, and managing requirements

- *User acceptance.* Managing requirements verification and validation activities (e.g., the user acceptance test)

- *Organizational readiness.* Preparing the organization for deployment of a new business solution

- *Staff augmentation.* Providing resources to augment project teams to perform business analysis activities that are under-resourced or urgent

- *Full-cycle governance.* Promotes a full-life-cycle governance process, managing investments in business solutions from research and development to operations. Provides a home (funding and resources) for pre-project business analysis and business case development. Activities include:

- *Business program management.* Works with management and the portfolio management team to implement a twenty-first-century model that transitions organizations from stand-alone IT project management to business program management.

□ *Strategic project resources.* Provides senior-level business analysts to lead the business analysis effort for strategic initiatives.

□ *Enterprise analysis.* Provides process coordination and meeting facilitation to the portfolio management team. Conducts enterprise analysis activities. Prepares the project investment decision package consisting of the business case, the results of studies, and other supporting information that provides senior management with a clear understanding of what business results are to be achieved through a major investment, including the contribution from IT to those results.

□ *Benefits management.* Measures the business benefits achieved by new business solutions; facilitates the adoption of a shared vision of the benefits realization process, managing the investment throughout the project life cycle and after the solution has been delivered. Ensures that the total cost of ownership (TCO) is understood and measured. TCO is the full life cycle product cost, including the cost to build or buy, deploy, support, maintain, and service the solution in both the business and the IT operations.

Although the BACoE is by definition *business focused*, it is of paramount importance for successful CoEs to operate in an environment where business operations and IT are aligned and in sync. It's also important to integrate the disciplines of project management, software engineering, and business analysis.

One of the key goals of organizational change management is to combine the change efforts that affect a business process under one coordinated initiative. Consider the potential changes that most organizations are undergoing concurrently:

- The *executive team* might be attempting to implement or improve a portfolio management process to select, prioritize, resource, and manage critical strategic projects. In addition, management might be implementing a new corporate scorecard to measure organizational performance.

- For enterprise-wide projects that affect several business units, some or all of the *business units* might be implementing improvements to the same business processes that will be modified by the larger change initiative.

- The *IT application development and infrastructure groups* might be undergoing large-scale change, such as implementing a SOA. Or, the *IT application group* might be implementing a different software development life cycle methodology, such as the Rational Unified Process (RUP) or Agile development.

- The *IT infrastructure support team* might be implementing the Information Technology Infrastructure Library (ITIL), an internationally recognized best practice framework for the delivery of quality IT Service Management (ITSM).

- The *IT enterprise architects* might be implementing a new framework to develop the business, information, technology, application, and security architectures.

- The *PMO* might be implementing a new project management methodology or tool.

These change initiatives must somehow be coordinated to optimize the return on the improvement efforts. CoEs that support centralized, full-cycle governance provide the framework for the benefits realization process from project conception to benefit harvesting. Centralized governance also provides a process of progressive resource commitment in which resources are allocated to programs in small increments through stage gates. It stands to reason then, that a centralized CoE would improve the management and coordination of strategic change initiatives.

One of the biggest challenges for the BACoE is to bridge the gap that divides business and IT. To do so, the BACoE must deliver multidimensional services to diverse groups. Regardless of whether there is one CoE or several more narrowly focused models, the CoE organization should be centralized.

BACoE Organizational Positioning Considerations

Organizational positioning usually equates with organizational authority. In other words, the higher a BACoE is positioned, the more autonomy, authority, and responsibility it is likely to have. According to Dennis Bolles, PMP, in *Building Project Management Centers of Excellence*, positioning the BACoE at the highest level possible provides the "measure of autonomy necessary to extend the authority across the organization while substantiating the value and importance the function has in the eyes of executive management."[6] In the absence of high-level positioning, the success and impact of the center will likely be significantly diminished.

Consider Figure 8-2, a model to centralize a CoE integrating the project management, business analysis, and quality assurance disciplines.

Understanding the business drivers behind the establishment of the CoE is of paramount importance. The motive behind establishing the center must be unambiguous because the motive will serve as the foundation to establish the purpose, objectives, scope, and functions of the center.

For example, the desire to set up a BACoE might have originated in IT, because of the number of strategic, mission-critical IT projects affecting the whole organization, or in a particular business area that is experiencing a significant level of change. Whatever the genesis,

Figure 8-2—Organizational Integration for CoEs

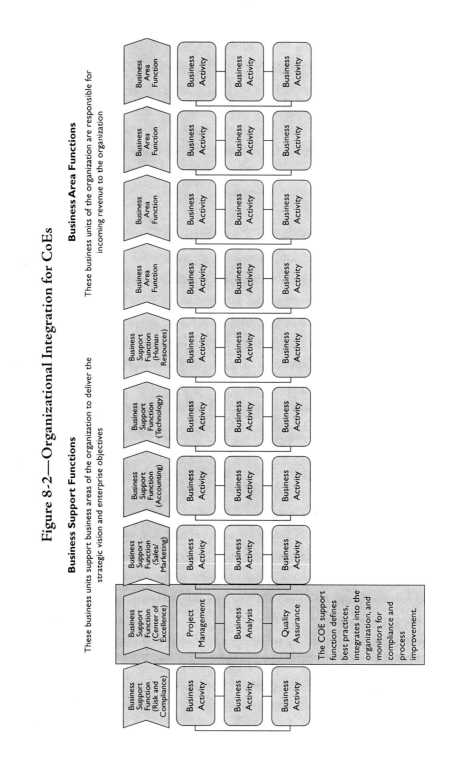

Business Support Functions

These business units support business areas of the organization to deliver the strategic vision and enterprise objectives

Business Area Functions

These business units of the organization are responsible for incoming revenue to the organization strive to place the center so that it serves the entire enterprise, not just IT or a particular business area.

Regardless of the CoE model or organizational positioning, the center's performance depends on the maturity of the organization's practices.

BACoE Organizational Maturity Considerations

The centralized CoE model is important, as are the effectiveness of the strategic planning and project portfolio management practices, the business performance management processes and strategies, the maturity of the IT architecture, the maturity of development and support processes, and the strength of the business focus across the enterprise.

Higher maturity levels are directly correlated to more effective procedures, higher quality deliverables, lower project costs, higher project team morale, a better balance between cost, schedule and scope, and ultimately improved profits for the organization. Organizations that understand the value of more mature practices achieve higher levels of value from their CoEs.

BACoE Implementation Considerations

Organizations can absorb a limited amount of concurrent change while maintaining productivity at any given time. Therefore, a gradual approach to implementing the BACoE is recommended. One option is to adopt a three-phased approach moving across the BACoE maturity continuum from a project-focused structure to a strategic organizational model. Figure 8-3 depicts the BACoE Maturity Model.

Project-centric

BACoEs are almost always project-centric in their early, formative phase. The goals of the BACoE at this stage are to build the confi-

Figure 8-3—BACoE Maturity Model

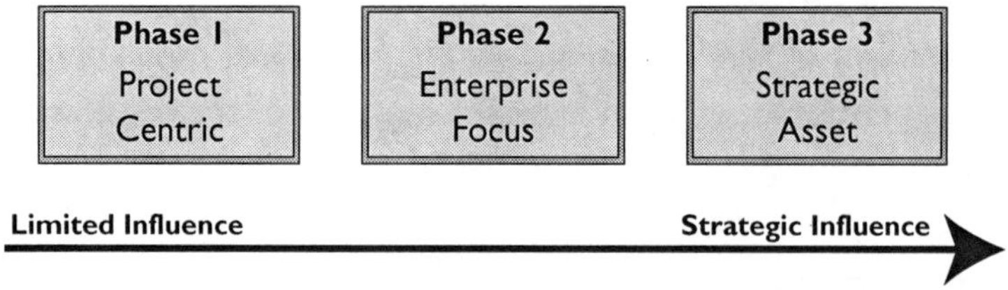

Phase 1	Phase 2	Phase 3
Project Centric	Enterprise Focus	Strategic Asset

Limited Influence → **Strategic Influence** ➤

---

dence of and become an indispensable resource to the project teams. During this early phase, the BACoE builds trusting relationships with business analysts, project managers, functional managers, and project teams. In addition to developing business analysis practice standards, the BACoE provides services to the project teams, as well as training and mentoring to develop business analysts and high-performing project teams.

Enterprise-Focused

As the BACoE begins to win confidence across the organization, it is likely that it will evolve into an enterprise-wide resource serving the entire company. At this point, the BACoE begins to facilitate the implementation of an effective portfolio management system. It is building the foundation to serve as a strategic business asset providing management with decision-support information.

Strategic

During the third stage of development, the BACoE is considered a strategic asset serving the executive team. At this point, it is well understood that business analysis has a positive effect on profitability and that organizations achieve strategic goals through well-prioritized, well-executed projects. Emphasis at this stage is placed on achieving professionalism in business analysis through the BACoE.

Strategic activities for the BACoE include: conducting research and providing the executive team with accurate competitive information, identifying and recommending viable new business opportunities, and preparing the project investment decision package to facilitate project selection and prioritization.

BACoE Implementation Best Practices

Although there are relatively few BACoEs in existence today, best practices for developing organizational CoEs to manage the business analysis function are emerging. Through a rational and defined methodology, organizations are identifying the required business analysis knowledge, skills, and abilities, assessing their current business analysis capabilities, and assembling a team to create the new entity.

Best practices for establishing CoEs combine to form a relatively standard process with four basic steps:

1. Define the center's vision and concept.

2. Conduct organizational and individual assessments.

3. Establish implementation plans.

4. Finalize planning and form BACoE action teams to develop and implement the center's infrastructure.

Figure 8-4 depicts the BACoE Implementation Model.

Define Vision and Concept

During the early study phase, it is important to create a vision for the new center. This is accomplished by researching the BACoEs that have already been implemented in organizations; studying their costs, benefits, strengths, and weaknesses; and determining lessons learned.

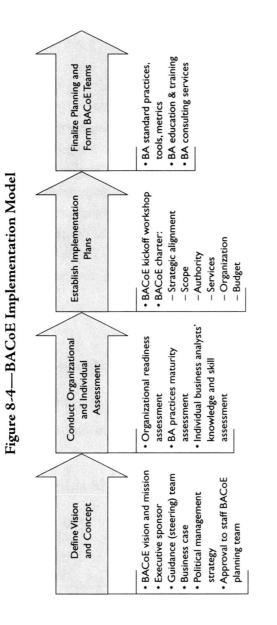

Figure 8-4—BACoE Implementation Model

Create a preliminary vision and mission statement for the center, and develop the concept in enough detail to prepare a *business case* for establishing the center. Vet the proposal with key stakeholders, and secure approval to form a small core team to conduct the assessment of business analysis practices and plan for the implementation of the BACoE.

Key stakeholders include: the executive enlisted as the BACoE executive sponsor, directors of existing CoEs in the organization, including the PMO if it exists, the CIO and IT management team, and executive directors and managers of business units undergoing significant change.

During meetings with the key stakeholders, secure buy-in and support for the concept. Large-scale organizational change of this nature typically involves restructuring, cultural transformation, new technologies, and forging new partnerships. Handling change well can mean the difference between success and failure of the effort.

In his book, *The Heart of Change*, John Kotter describes the techniques to consider during the early study and planning phase, including:[7]

+ *Executive sponsorship.* A CoE cannot exist successfully without an executive sponsor. Build a trusting, collaborative relationship with the sponsor, seeking mentoring and coaching at every turn.

+ *Political management strategy.* Conduct an analysis of key stakeholders to determine those that can influence the center, and whether they feel positively or negatively about the center. Identify the goals of the key stakeholders. Assess the political environment. Define problems, solutions, and action plans to take advantage of positive influences and to neutralize negative ones.

+ *A sense of urgency.* Work with stakeholder groups to reduce complacency, fear, and anger over the change, and to increase their sense of urgency.

+ *The guiding team.* Build a team of supporters that have the credibility, skills, connections, reputations, and formal authority to provide the necessary leadership to help shape the BACoE.

+ *The vision.* Use the guiding team to develop a clear, simple, compelling vision for the BACoE and a set of strategies to achieve the vision.

+ *Communication for buy-in.* Execute a simple, straightforward communication plan using forceful and convincing messages sent through many channels. Use the guiding team to promote the vision whenever possible.

+ *Empowerment for action.* Use the guiding team to remove barriers to change, including disempowering management styles, antiquated business processes, and inadequate information.

+ *Short-term wins.* Wins create enthusiasm and momentum. Plan the implementation to achieve early successes.

+ *Dependency management.* The success of the center is likely dependent on coordination with other groups in the organization. Assign someone from your core team as the *dependency owner*, to liaise with each dependent group. A best practice is for dependency owners to attend team meetings of the dependent group to demonstrate the importance of the relationship and to solicit feedback and recommendations for improvements.

Conduct Organizational and Individual Assessments

It is imperative to understand the current state of the organization before building BACoE implementation plans. Once the current state is understood and documented, it may be necessary to refine the vision and mission of the CoE to ensure alignment with cultural readiness of the organization to embrace the new CoE.

Organizational Readiness Assessment

The purpose of the organizational readiness assessment is to determine organizational expectations for the BACoE and to gauge the cultural readiness for the change. The BACoE assessment team determines where the organization is on the continuum from a stovepipe, function-centric structure to an enterprise-focused organization. Additionally, it is useful to gather information about best practices already in place in the organization that might serve as a springboard for replication across projects.

The assessment also provides the BACoE planning team with information on key challenges, gaps, and issues that the BACoE should address immediately. The ideal assessment solution is to conduct a formal organizational maturity assessment. A less formal assessment, however, may suffice at this point.

As soon as the concept has been approved and the core BACoE implementation team is in place, conduct an assessment to understand and document the current state of business analysis practices. The assessment consists of interviews with functional managers, business analysts, project managers, and IT professionals. The goal is to determine whether the organization is ready to establish such a center, and to assess the current state of the following entities:

+ *Business analysts.* The individuals currently involved in business analysis practices. Particularly, the assessment inquires about their knowledge, skills, experience, roles, responsibilities, organizational placement, training, professional development opportunities, and career path. The assessment also notes any other duties assigned to the business analysts, their measures of success, and performance evaluations.

+ *Business analysis practices.* Formal and informal business analysis methodologies and techniques, including feasibility study processes, business case development processes, business architecture development standards or framework, requirements elicitation, analysis, specification, validation, and change management processes, requirements prioritization and traceability methods, requirements verification (user acceptance test) methods, and any other business analysis tools, templates, and guidelines.

+ *Technology.* Requirements development and archiving tools, including powerful modeling tools, requirements repository and management systems, and team collaboration tools.

+ *Governance.* Oversight for project selection and prioritization, and ongoing reviews of BA practices. Quality assurance functions to ensure compliance with BA standards. A portfolio management team to select and prioritize projects. Benefits management throughout the project and after solution delivery.

Formal Organizational Maturity Assessment

If the organization is going to invest in a formal maturity assessment, we recommend conducting an assessment that determines not only the state of business analysis but also the state of project management and software engineering practices to secure a complete picture of program and project maturity. The CompassBA/PM™ Organizational Maturity Model (CompassBA/PM™ OMM) was developed by Management Concepts to focus on improving both project management and business analysis practices, thus ensuring compatibility and alignment with the de facto standards available in the information technology (IT) project improvement arena.

The CompassBA/PM™ OMM is a staged maturity model similar to those used by several standard-setting bodies. The model is mapped to industry standards by establishing specific business analysis, project management, and software engineering practice goals to be achieved to reach advanced levels of the model. Refer to Figure 8-5 for a graphical depiction of the CompassBA/PM™ OMM.

The power of the CompassBA/PM™ OMM comes from integrating the following resources:

- The project management knowledge areas described in PMI's *Guide to the Project Management Body of Knowledge (PMBOK® Guide)*, 3rd ed., including the project management areas defined by its knowledge requirements and described in terms of its component processes, practices, inputs, outputs, tools and techniques

- The key practices embodied in the IIBA *Business Analysis Body of Knowledge (BABOK™ Guide)* described in terms of key practices and techniques

- The *SEI Capability Maturity Model® Integration (CMMI)* selected software and system engineering process areas representing a group of best practices that, when performed collectively, satisfy a set of goals considered important for making significant improvement in that process area

Individual Knowledge and Skill Assessments

It is also important to determine the skill level of existing business analysts (and project managers, if appropriate). The *Compass-BA/PM—Individual™* assessment, also developed by Management Concepts, is a formal capabilities assessment of business analysts and project managers. The assessment results provide the basis for determining training requirements, professional development activi-

Figure 8-5—The CompassBA/PM™ OMM

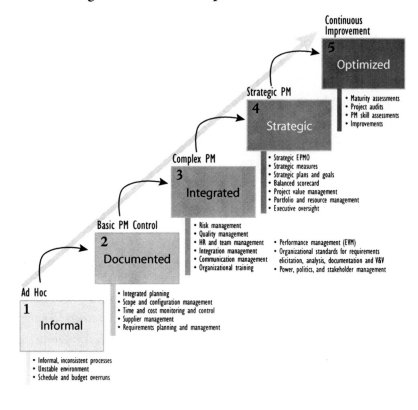

ties, and specific mentoring and coaching needs. As with the organizational assessment, the individual assessment benchmarks an individual business analyst or project manager against the industry standards, the *PMBOK® Guide* and the *BABOK™ Guide*.

Establish Implementation Plans

The BACoE kickoff workshop serves as the capstone event that officially launches the BACoE. All key stakeholders should attend to participate in decision-making discussions about the new BACoE.

In preparation for the workshop, develop a preliminary charter and business plan for the center, describing the center's key elements.

Conduct a BACoE kickoff workshop session to finalize the charter and plans and to gain consensus on an implementation approach. Refer to Table 8-1 for a detailed list of planning considerations.

Table 8-1—CoE Planning Considerations

Planning Considerations	Description
Strategic alignment, vision, and mission	Present the case for the BACoE and reference the business case for more detailed information about cost versus benefits of the center.
Assessment results	Include or reference the results of the assessments that were conducted: • Maturity of the business analysis practices • Summary of the skill assessments • Recommendations, including training and professional development of business analysts and improvement of business analysis practice standards
Scope	Describe the scope of BACoE responsibilities, including: • The professional disciplines (PM/BA) guided by the center • The functions the center will perform • The processes the center will standardize, monitor, and continuously improve • The metrics that will be tracked to determine the success of the center
Authority	CoEs can be purely advisory, or they can have the authority to own and direct business processes. Organizational placement should be commensurate with the authority and role of the center. When describing the authority of the CoE, include the governance structure—to whom the CoE will report for guidance and approval of activities.
Services	A CoE is almost always a resource center, developing and maintaining information on best practices and lessons learned, and assigning business analysts to projects. Document the proposed role: • Materials (e.g., reference articles, templates, job aids, tools, procedures, methods, practices) • Services (e.g., business case development, portfolio management team support, consulting, mentoring, standards development, quality reviews, workshop facilitators, allotting resources to project teams)

Table 8-1—CoE Planning Considerations (continued)

Planning Considerations	Description
Organization	Describe the BACoE team structure, management, and operations including: • Positions and their roles, responsibilities, and knowledge and skill requirements • Reporting relationships • Linkages to other organizational entities
Budget and Staffing Levels	At a high level, describe the proposed budget, including facilities, tools and technology, and staffing ramp-up plans.
Implementation Approach	Document the formation of initial action teams that will begin building the foundational elements of the center. Describe the organizational placement of the center, and its initial focus (e.g., project-centric, enterprise-centric, strategically focused).

Finalize Planning and Form BACoE Teams

After the workshop session, finalize the BACoE charter and staff the center. Form action teams to develop business analysis practice standards. Provide education, training, mentoring, and consulting support. Secure the needed facilities, tools, and supplies. Figure 8-6 shows a typical BACoE organization.

Develop the *BACoE Business Plan/Operations Guide*, describing implementation strategy, phases, deliverables, milestones, and a detailed budget, listing salaries and training, technology, and consulting costs. The guide should also list infrastructure requirements, acquisition, installation, BACoE organization formation, initial orientation and training, and communications and risk management plans.

Final Words of Wisdom

Establishing CoEs is difficult because doing so destabilizes the sense of balance and power within the organization. Executives are required to make decisions based on benefits to the enterprise versus their specific functional areas. Functional managers are often afraid of losing their authority and control over the resources as-

Figure 8-6—Typical BACoE Organization

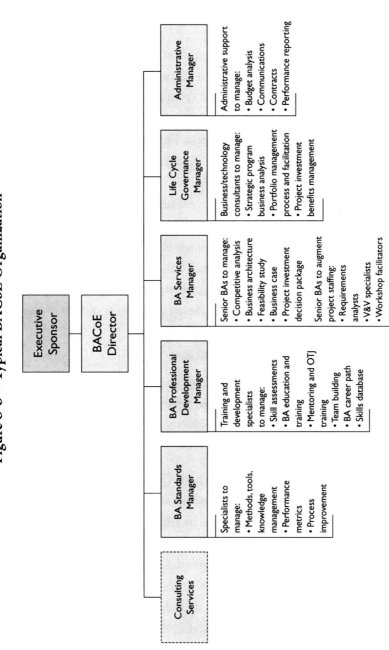

signed to them. In addition, project team members might be unclear about their roles and responsibilities, and how they will be given assignments.

These ambiguities might manifest themselves as resistance to change and will pose a risk to a successful implementation. Therefore, it is imperative that robust coordination and effective communication about how the center will affect roles and responsibilities accompany center implementation. Do not underestimate such challenges. Pay close attention to organizational change management strategies and use them liberally.

To establish a BACoE that executives love and project teams trust, make the center indispensable. Provide high-quality services and support to executives, management, and project teams rather than imposing requirements and constraints. Conduct the operations of the center and design business analysis practices using lean techniques. Follow this motto: *Barely sufficient is enough to move on.*

Providing Value to the Organization

To establish a BACoE that lasts, you must be able to demonstrate the value the center brings to the organization. Develop measures of success and report progress to executives to demonstrate that value. Typical measures of success include:

+ *Project cost overrun reduction.* Quantify the project time and cost overruns prior to the implementation of the BACoE and for the projects supported by the BACoE. If an organizational baseline measurement is not available, use industry standard benchmarks as a comparison. Other measures might be improvements to team member morale and reduction in project staff turnover. Be sure to include opportunity costs caused by the delayed implementation of the new solution.

+ *Project time and cost savings.* Track the number of requirements defects discovered during testing and after the solution is in production before and after the implementation of the BACoE. Quantify the value in terms of reduced rework costs and improved customer satisfaction.

+ *Project portfolio value.* Prepare reports for the executive team that provide the investment costs and expected value of the portfolio of projects; report the actual value new solutions add to the organization as compared to the expected value predicted in the business case. When calculating cost, be sure to use the total cost of ownership, including the cost to build or buy, deploy, support, maintain, and service the solution in both business and IT operations.

Building a Great Team

When staffing the BACoE, establish a small, mighty *core team* dedicated full-time to the center, co-located, highly trained, and multiskilled. Do not overstaff the center because the cost will seem prohibitive. Augment the core team's efforts by bringing in subject matter experts and forming sub-teams as needed. Select team members not only because of their knowledge and skills but also because they are passionate and love to work in a challenging, collaborative environment. Develop and use a team operating agreement. Develop team-leadership skills and dedicate efforts to transition the group into a high-performing team with common values, beliefs, and a cultural foundation upon which to flourish.

Endnotes

1. Jonathan G. Geiger. "Intelligent Solutions: Establishing a Center of Excellence," *BI Review Newsletter*, March 20, 2007. Online at http://www.bireview.com/article.cfm?articleid=222 (accessed March 29, 2007).

2. Mark Frederick Davis. *SOA: Providing Flexibility for the Health and Science Industry*, July 2006. Online at http://h20247.www2.hp.com/publicsector/downloads/Technology_Davis_VB.pdf (accessed March 29, 2007).

3. Chris Andrews. *IBM Initiative to Capture New Growth Opportunities in Information Management*, February 16, 2006. Online at http://www-03.ibm.com/press/us/en/pressrelease/19249.wss (accessed March 29, 2007).

4. SAP America, Inc., *2006 USAG/SAP Best Practices Survey: Centers of Excellence: Optimize Your Business and IT Value*, February 16, 2007. Online at http://whitepapers.zdnet.com/whitepaper.aspx?&docid=284768&promo=100510 (accessed March 28, 2007).

5. Kathleen Barret gave a presentation on the successful Bank of Montreal center of excellence at a Business Analysis World conference in Washington D.C. in June 2006. For more information on Business Analysis World symposium series and other events, go to http://www.businessanalystworld.com/ (accessed August 23, 2007).

6. Dennis Bolles. *Building Project Management Centers of Excellence*, 2002. New York: American Management Association.

7. John P. Kotter and Dan Cohen. *The Heart of Change*, 2002. Boston: Harvard Business School Press.

Epilogue

Effective business analysis is a critical link to help organizations meet business needs, improve customer service, and maximize the return on project investments. It is no wonder that business analysts everywhere are increasingly expanding out of traditional, technical roles into leadership roles that share responsibility for the success of the project. Indeed, if you are a business analyst reading this book, it is very likely that your organization is expecting you to take on an elevated project leadership role.

This book will help you fulfill that role. Part II, for example, presented three key competencies that you as a business analyst must add to your technical skill set to be successful as a project leader: teamwork, communication and customer relationship management. Applying these skills on projects that encompass large-scale organizational change efforts will help you perform effectively as a strategic implementer, build a high-performing team, and prepare the organization to accept the new business solution.

An important next step after reading this book is for you to participate in a business analysis competency assessment to evaluate not only your business analysis competencies, such as requirements planning and analysis, but your general management, leadership, and project management competencies as well.

The results of a baseline competency assessment will help you identify opportunities for improvement and strengths on which to build your project leadership capabilities. As described in Chapter 3, the business analysis competency assessment should cover key skills and competencies across the business solutions life cycle and be mapped to a project leadership career path. Compare your current competency level with the industry competency benchmark for your position.

The results of your competency assessment should provide an indication of whether your current skill level aligns with your current project responsibilities. If you are working on large, highly complex projects, leadership skills are critical, so it's imperative to seek out training and development efforts to enhance these skills.

Business analysis competency assessments, in general, are used by organizations to foster training and professional development efforts. Unfortunately, what most assessments deliver is a long list of opportunities for improvement and the associated training courses to address each area. A missing component of these assessments is guidance on which actions the business analyst should implement first, and which actions will make the most difference in the current workplace.

If you have participated in one of these assessments, you can use the results to help you prioritize the training and development efforts that will result in the most immediate improvement in your project performance. The more complex your projects, the more leadership responsibility you will most likely have to assume. Remember, building leadership potential requires a diverse development plan that includes training, mentoring, networking, participating in professional associations, and expanding project opportunities.

Organizations must commit to enhancing their business analysis maturity, too. To achieve business analysis and project management success, organizations often need to change their management systems. This does not mean trying to make drastic personnel changes or applying a one-step solution. Rather, organizations should establish conditions that enable people to work together effectively, with mutual trust. This creates an opportunity for the full expression of accountability, authority, and creativity in managing projects.[1]

It is a long-term commitment for organizations to increase business analysis and project management maturity, because maturity typically progresses gradually and iteratively over time. Even if an organization follows a defined capability maturity model, it should expect false starts and relatively unsuccessful organizational improvement efforts at first.

Organizations tend to default to training when they want to improve the skills of their business analysts, but they often fail to realize that training alone may not provide the most performance improvement. If organizational support systems aren't available to actually *apply* training concepts in the workplace, training alone won't bring about intended improvements.

A business analyst center of excellence (BACoE) can help the organization continue improvement momentum, as described in Chapter 8. Similar to the project management office (PMO), the BACoE serves as a strategic asset to promote project collaboration, build business analysis skill levels, and reinforce the application of business analysis best practices on projects.

As you carve out your leadership role and begin to influence executives, you can encourage your organization to build additional components into its capability maturity plan to help you practice what you learn in training. Without this support, you will experience an increase in your knowledge and skill level personally, but your project performance outcomes may still be less than what is expected. This causes a gap between your current potential capability and current applied capability, and your projects may suffer as a result.

When you have difficulty applying business analysis and leadership skills on projects, it may be due to this capability gap. If so, it is important for you to understand the cause of the gap, whether it be lack of personal skill or obstacles in the organizational environment. Gaps caused by either situation create a range of personal feelings from resignation, apathy, and despondency to activism, motivation, and productive engagement as a change agent. A highly skilled business analyst, for example, who is unable to effectively apply his or her skills in the organization because of a lack of management support, may eventually experience resignation or apathy because he or she has limited ability to control project outcomes.

Despite any deficiency in the training maturity of your organization, strive to continue to build your personal effectiveness by developing your own *self-efficacy*—believing that your own knowledge, skills, and experience will enable you to achieve the defined project goals. Seek (or try to create) an organizational environment that is responsive and rewards valued accomplishments, fosters aspirations and productive engagement in activities, and provides a sense of fulfillment.[2] When a competent business analyst works in this type of environment, he or she is able to exercise substantial control over project responsibilities and professional development activities.

Your belief in your self-efficacy is critical to adaptive functioning and affects how you think, motivate yourself, feel, and behave.[3] But your feelings of self-efficacy are influenced by a general expectation: your actions determine outcomes, or external forces beyond your control determine outcomes.

The belief about whether your actions affect outcomes is called *locus of control*. For example, an experienced business analyst with high self-efficacy who works in an organizational environment that rewards and supports project management will most likely feel like he or she has control over project outcomes. The business analyst will perform at a higher level of competence, gain personal satisfaction from performing work, and aspire to continuous improvement. The same business analyst in an unsupportive environment may initially intensify his or her efforts to make a difference in the organization, but when the organization does not respond, the business analyst may become frustrated and leave the organization, or change his or her performance expectations to work within the system.

The key message here is that as a business analyst and as a leader, you must take control of your own career development and work environment to minimize the gap between current potential capability and current applied capability. Building competence in your leadership skills and applying these skills on projects will help you develop and sustain a level of credibility that will drive change and maturity in your organization.

Make a commitment to increase your business analysis leadership self-efficacy by taking control of your training and development efforts, seeking out opportunities to effectively apply your skills, and negotiating for what you need to align your level of competence with the complexity of your projects.

The key is to take control of those things you can. Improve your locus of control by understanding the cause of the gap between your current potential capability and current applied capability. Establish a BACoE to influence the direction of business analysis and project management maturity in your organization. Educate your middle and senior managers on the value of effective business analysis and project management by exhibiting business-outcome thinking, developing creative solutions and options, providing vision and direction for projects, facilitating stakeholder collaboration, and contributing to the establishment of business analysis best practices in your organization. Are you up for the challenge?

Lori Lindbergh

Endnotes

1. Elliott Jacques. *Requisite Organization: A Total System for Effective Managerial Organization and Managerial Leadership for the 21st Century*, 1998. Arlington, VA: Cason Hall & Company Publishers.

2. Albert Bandura. *Self-Efficacy: The Exercise of Control*, 1997. New York: W. H. Freeman and Company.

3. Ibid.

Index

CPSIA information can be obtained at www.ICGtesting.com
Printed in the USA
BVOW032323080312

284701BV00005B/1/P